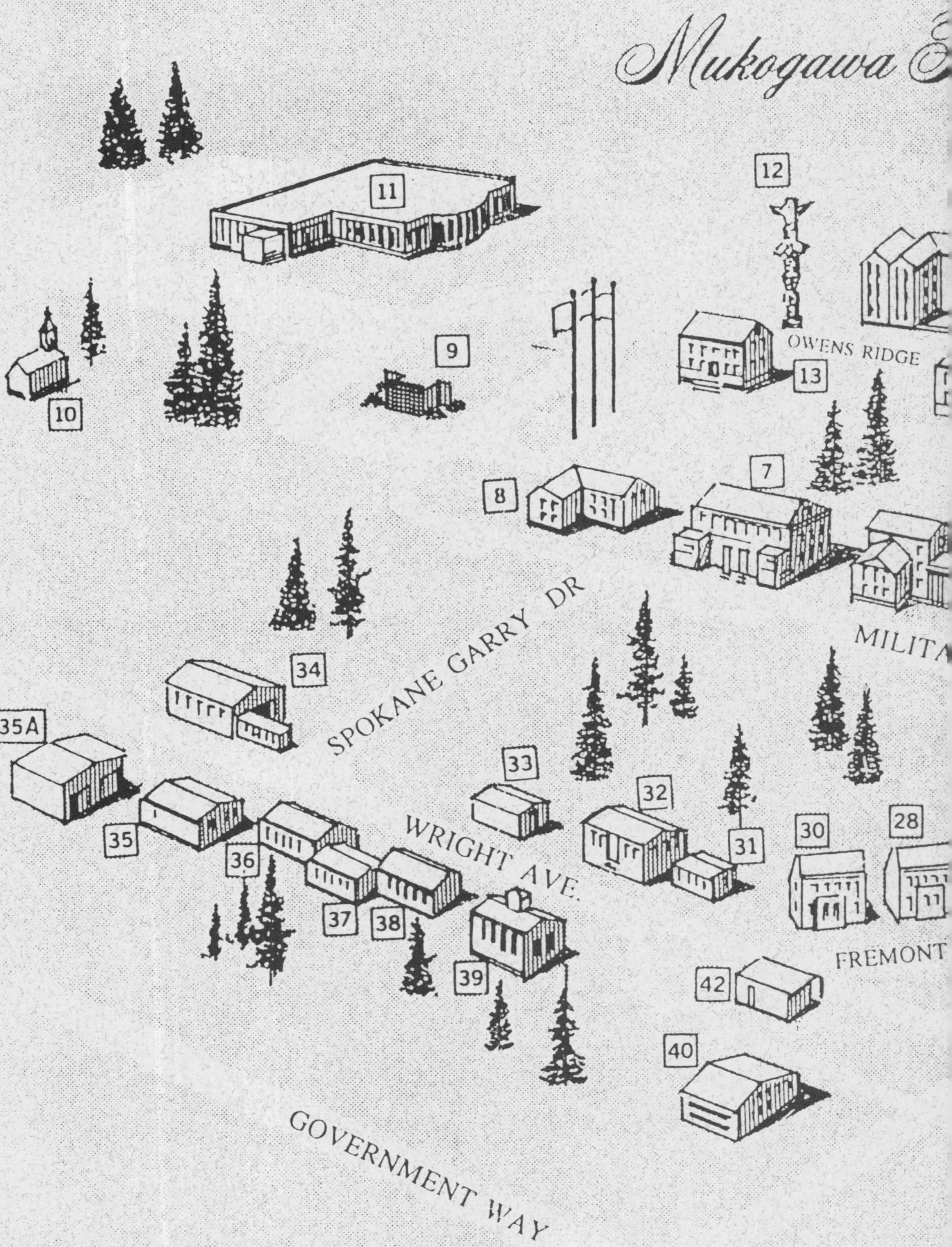

4000 WEST RANDOLPH ROAD
SPOKANE, WASHINGTON 99204
PHONE (509) 328-2971 (FOOD SERVICE 327-3441)
FAX (509) 325-6540

Fort Wright Institute

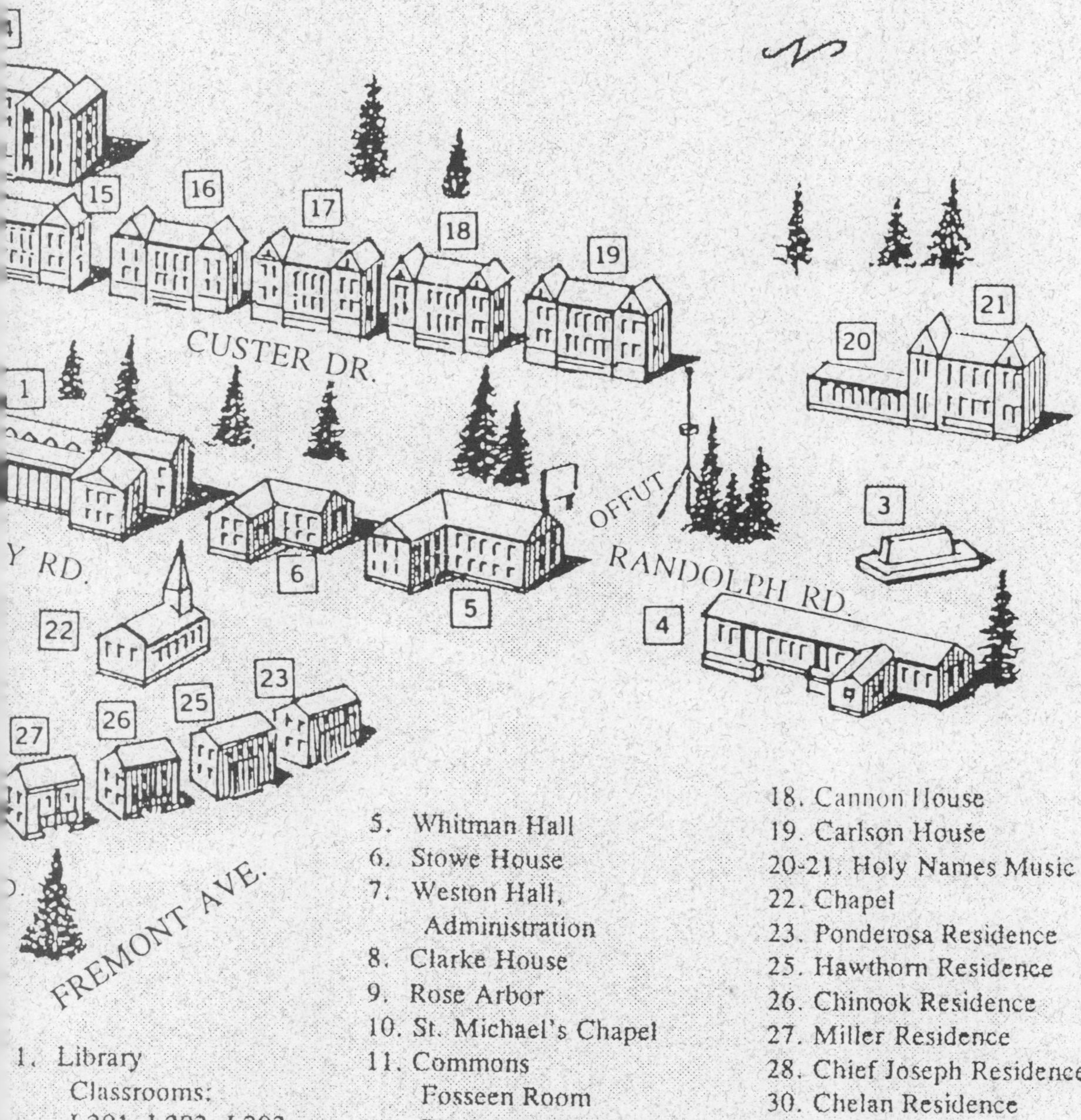

1. Library
   Classrooms:
   L201, L202, L203
   Audio Visual Room
   Computer Room
   Faculty Offices
3. Monument
4. Greystones
   Japanese C.C.
   Classrooms: CC1,2

5. Whitman Hall
6. Stowe House
7. Weston Hall,
   Administration
8. Clarke House
9. Rose Arbor
10. St. Michael's Chapel
11. Commons
   Fosseen Room
   Regents & Banquet Rooms
   Student Dining Hall
12. Totem Pole
13. Nellie Garry Guest Hse.
14. Covington Hall
15. Cather House
16. Dickinson House
17. Helen Keller House

18. Cannon House
19. Carlson House
20-21. Holy Names Music Ctr.
22. Chapel
23. Ponderosa Residence
25. Hawthorn Residence
26. Chinook Residence
27. Miller Residence
28. Chief Joseph Residence
30. Chelan Residence
31. Paint Shop
32. Toddler House
33. Art Gallery
34-35. Maintenance
36-38. MacDonald Clsrm. Bldg.
39. Stanton Classroom Bldg.
40. Montessori
42. Gas Station

FORT GEORGE WRIGHT:

NOT ONLY WHERE THE BAND PLAYED

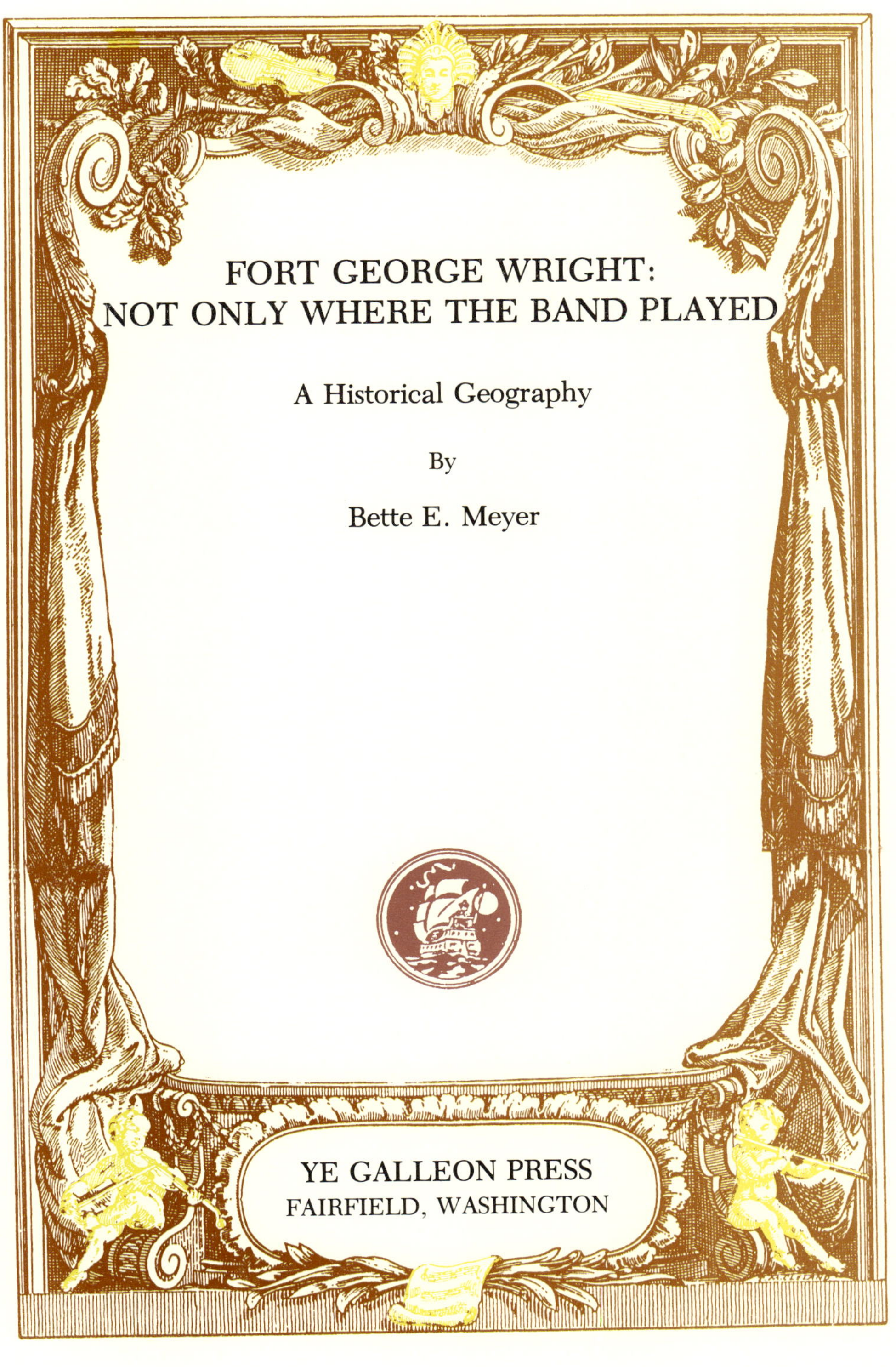

FORT GEORGE WRIGHT:
NOT ONLY WHERE THE BAND PLAYED

A Historical Geography

By

Bette E. Meyer

YE GALLEON PRESS
FAIRFIELD, WASHINGTON

Library of Congress Cataloging-in-Publication Data

Meyer, Bette Eunice.
　　Fort George Wright : not only where the band played / by Bette
E. Meyer.
　　　　p.　cm.
　　Includes bibliographical references and index.

　　　ISBN 0-87770-525-9 (pb)
　　　ISBN 0-87770-543-7

　　　1. Fort George Wright (Wash.) — History.　2. Spokane (Wash.)
— History. I Title.
F899.S7M5　　　　　　1994　　　　　979.7'37-dc20　　　　　94-32422

TABLE OF CONTENTS

INTRODUCTION

During my employment at Holy Names Center at Fort Wright as Development Director and Marketing Co-ordinator, I received many inquiries about Fort George Wright from visitors. I quickly realized I knew very little about the site and began to remedy the situation by conducting some research. My intention was to prepare a one page hand-out which would cover basic information to satisfy most of the questions posed by visitors.

My investigation may have satisfied visitors inquiries but it did not satisfy me. Information gathered led to more questions in my mind that demanded answers. My subsequent intention was to develop the one page hand-out and perhaps a short article — for publication, with the possibility of re-prints for sale at Holy Names Center for those who might have more interest in the topic. The Center needed any and all income for its budget.

Before long my research produced much more information than could be reasonably contained in an article. This small book is the result.

This book is by no means meant to be a definitive study of Fort George Wright, either as an historical geography or as an in-depth study. Rather, it is an attempt to share information I have acquired. There is little data available in popular or readily available sources that treat other than isolated topics relative to Fort George Wright.

Preparing this book was an enjoyable adventure. I hope you will enjoy reading it.

Bette E. Meyer

great boon to Spokane's economic woes, securing the post was not a simple matter, for many other communities were quick to understand the advantages of the Army in their midst.[2]

Well aware that a military garrison would infuse large amounts of cash into the region's economy and attract new business in addition, city officials instructed businessmen William S. Norman, W.J. Dyer, and Albert A. Newberry to try to obtain the army post for the city. They bonded a site of 2000 acres on Peone Prairie, just north of Spokane, as an option for the fort, and then sent the city's proposal to the War Department.[3]

Despite this offer from the community, nothing happened until Albert Newberry went to the nation's capitol to discuss the situation with Secretary of War Daniel S. Lamont, who then arranged a meeting with General John. M. Scofield, commander of the United States Army. The Depression of 1893 made finances rather tight for the City of Spokane and in 1894 there were few funds readily available to send a lobbyist to Washington, D.C. Therefore, citizens took it upon themselves to raise the money that would permit Newberry to stay in Washington for several weeks. In the meetings between General Scofield and Newberry, the General set certain conditions which, if met, would then ensure that Spokane would be awarded the coveted Army post. Upon his return to Spokane, Newberry addressed a mass meeting at the downtown Auditorium Theatre and told his listeners that the Army's requirements included Spokane's donation of 1000 acres of land and the assurance of free water to the post. Officials suggested one hundred gallons per capita per day for drinking and domestic use.[4]

A committee formed from among those attending the Auditorium Theatre meeting to coordinate efforts to fulfill the Army's requirements. Selected for this group were respected men of means in the community, many of whom financed Newberry's stay in Washington, D.C. Their professional experience brought an efficient and effective character to the plans they proposed.

What the Army demands meant, essentially, was that the City of Spokane needed to raise approximately $15,000 in cash. Businessmen correctly theorized that the majority of the land for the fort site would be donated. Nonetheless, to obtain the large amount of money which would compensate those asked to give up property at the post site was an awesome task for a town where 15 cents was considered good money. In fact, most of the people walked home from the meeting at the Auditorium Theatre the evening of Newberry's report because they did not have the fare for the streetcars.

About the time that Spokane actively pursued the Army in order to persuade Army Brass to locate the proposed fort in the city, Brigadier General Elwell Otis, the commander of the Army's Department of the Columbia, declared that "neither Fort Spokane nor Fort Sherman satisfies conditions which should determine permanance . . . . The two garrisons should be united at some more convenient point . . . The city of Spokane is . . . . the proper location." The Center for Military History records quoted General Otis as remarking that he "considered it of great importance that this tract of land be accepted at once. . . ." In this he echoed the sentiments of his predecessor, Brigadier General Carlin who, in the fall of 1893 recommended that Fort Spokane be discontinued and that a military post be built near Spokane.

Colonel Robert H. Hall had inspected the proposed location with First Lieutenant James A. Leyden, 4th Infantry, implementing Special Orders No. 179, and filed his positive report on December 1, 1894. He indicated that not only was the tract suitable but in many particulars it was most desirable. Colonel Hall observed that the site would be appropriate for "four troops of cavalry and a battery of light artillery," composed of 1200 to 1500 men. A week later, General Otis endorsed action on Colonel Hall's report; two days after that General Scofield recommended the site for the construction of the post. The bill to establish the fort became law on February 12, 1895.[5]

General Otis considered several locations when he had visited the city in the spring of 1894. These included one on the east end of the city, another in Cook's Addition (near Division and 14th), one north of Lidgerwood, and the Twickenham site, the latter being preferred by the General. In mid-December, 1894 Washington Congressman John L. Wilson (Rep.) added an amendment to the Appropriations Bill for the Army which authorized the Secretary of War to accept the Spokane location. Representative Wilson's amendment read as follows:

> That upon the transfer and conveyance to the United States of a good and sufficient title to not less that 1000 acres of land without cost to the United States, situated at or near the City of Spokane in the County of Spokane in the State of Washington, and on or near a railroad, and contributing an eligible and suitable site for an Army post, and to be approved and accepted by the Secretary of War is

hereby authorized to establish and locate on said land, a
United States Army post of such character and capacity as
the Secretary of War shall direct and approve.

The Bill was bitterly fought in the Senate, but through the efforts of
Senator Watson Squire of Washington and Senator Joseph C.S. Blackburn of
Kentucky, the measure ultimately passed the Senate, with the approval of
$100,000 in construction funds coming in June, 1896. Representative Samuel
C. Hyde (Rep.) of Spokane had attached an amendment to the Sundry Civil
Appropriations Bill in the spring which allocated $75,000 of $300,000
earmarked for building at military posts to the new post at Spokane for
beginning the construction of permanent buildings, water supply, sewerage,
roads, and other necessary facilities.[6]

Army officials saw several advantages to Spokane. The city was the
railroad center of the extreme Northwest, permitting troops stationed there to
be quickly sent in any direction to other localities in the United States or in the
Pacific. Besides being a healthy location with good water, the Army
determined that both construction and maintenance costs were lower in
Spokane than in other communities in the Pacific Northwest. The beauty of
the site not only favorably impressed Secretary of War Lamont but he also
liked the "thorough business-like way in which the Spokane people had
presented their proposition."[7]

Community officials viewed the proposed post in realistic and in patriotic
terms. On the one hand, they assumed that an adjacent Army installation
would serve as a "perpetual lesson in patriotism" and that the

> . . . constant display of the national colors . . . the
> booming of the sunset gun . . . the soldierly bearing of the
> men in uniform . . . would exert a fine influence on the
> rising generation . . . and keep fresh and beautiful the
> patriotic spirit of the people.[8]

On the other hand, mathematical calculations produced data that
indicated that the Army would initially spend about one-half million dollars in
Spokane. In addition, the monthly payroll of thousands of dollars and about
$5000 monthly for food — most of it coming from the Spokane region —
would bring more money to the area. These economic benefits from the

Army's presence were emphasized to all segments of the region, while the "social advantages, appealing only to the elite, were rarely mentioned."[9]

City officials further anticipated that this income would cancel all the indebtedness of the city, the county, and its citizens, and would "add $20 per capita of new money annually." With a thousand soldiers expected to be stationed at the post, city officialdom foresaw $21,000 circulating from their monthly wages alone. They also thought that one twenty-fifth of the entire United States Army would be posted at the Spokane garrison, and further theorized that many officers and men would elect to stay in Spokane when they retired. Not only would their half-pay retirement be welcomed but they would increase the city's population. In short, a military establishment in Spokane would stimulate economic growth and development far beyond normal expectations.[10]

Quite possibly, monetary hopes to relieve the tight financial situation brought about by the 1893 Panic and subsequent Depression motivated the City Fathers to develop plans which would meet the requirements outlined by the Army. City officials worked diligently to acquire property needed for the fort. Citizen sub-committees formed to address different segments of the task. The Army Post Executive Committee had as its responsibility the acquisition of the 1000 acres of land on which to erect the military establishment. Although it looked promising to have out-right donations or pledges to exchange land on the proposed military reservation for property of equally assessed evaluation in other parts of the city, the Committee realized that the major obstacle would be sufficient donations of cash and property so as to placate the owners who would be asked to relinquish property at the fort site. It was impossible to clear title to the 1000 acres until the full trading fund for compensation had been raised. To make honoring pledges and securing donations more attractive, the Spokane County Commissioners agreed to cancel back taxes on the fort property. The Army Post Committee stated that they would not expend one dollar for obtaining the fort until all pledges were paid and all cash was at hand. The Committee let it be known that delay could kill the entire project and stated that "if Spokane did not get the post, every dollar and every foot of land subscribed would be returned." Any surplus was to be distributed in proportion to the amount of the subscription.[11]

Setting an example for others to follow, the Fall City Land Company and the Washigton Water Power Company both donated 125 acres to the project. Attorneys J.W. Binkley and J.R. Taylor contributed $8000 worth of land and made a cash donation of $1000. H. B. Nichols gave $1000 and F. Lewis Clark doubled that amount. Albert P. Wolverton contributed $500. The Northern Pacific Railway gave a parcel of land.[12]

Concerned citizens introduced a number of schemes to raise funds for the enterprise. One consisted of a plan to have every wage-earner in the city donate a day's pay. Another plan involved a series of assessments for different classes of workers: $1000 for physicians; the same amount for lawyers; $250 for dentists; and $500 from employees and officials at the Courthouse. In the meantime, a group with visions of generous profits to be made should the Army award the post to Spokane — brewers and saloonkeepers — swung into gear. They were noted as working with "enthusiasm and vim" and were "chock full of public spirit."[13]

A variety of entertainments garnered money for the Army post project. A gala concert, staged at the Auditorium Theatre, was a great success. Theatre patrons came out in force and society ladies came in their prettiest gowns. For the event, some fifty people sold tickets, which were in great demand. Promoters held an auction for boxes at the theatre and a thirty-piece band, whose members donated their services to the City, played ten "masterpieces" during the evening's program.[14]

As the society event of the season, many wished to be associated with it. Florists donated their best flowers to enhance the stage. Fashionable ladies held pre-concert parties for special guests with whom they attended the gala, often in the highly prized theatre boxes. The concert committee did recommend, however, that "the ladies leave their bonnets at home or in the dressing room." Everyone attending wanted to see everything and everyone possible. The event cleared $1200 for the Fort Purchase Fund.[15]

Another fund raising program at the beautiful Auditorium Theatre was a Christmas Tree entertainment, proposed by Mrs. Alice Houghton. Citizens of the community wrote the names of musical numbers they wanted to hear at the concert; the Band played in the evening's program the compositions receiving the greatest number of votes. Surrounding the 20-foot Christmas Tree, adorned with colored lights and decorations of the season, were presents gathered from merchants and other donors in the area. Gifts ranged from a mounted deer head to 30 days of medical treatment to a full set of china. The one-dollar tickets for the entertainment admitted the holder to the theatre and guaranteed each person a present. Although the effects of the 1893 Panic and subsequent Depression were constant reminders to Spokane's citizens, the $1.00 tickets had "practically become legal tender around the city." The *Spokesman Review* editorialized that ". . . the public generally has greater confidence in their value than the proposed currency that Mr. Cleveland and Mr. Carlisle want the country to use." This well-attended unusual event garnered over $4500 for the Purchase Fund. Because every dollar helped, officials decided to auction those unclaimed prizes from the Christmas Tree Entertainment and concert. The auction took place prominently on the steps of the First National Bank Building in Spokane.[16]

Constructed at the turn of the century, the Bake House turned out all baked goods for the troops. The dough bins had to be replaced regularly.

This Quarter Master's workshops and warehouse reflected the architecture of the other post buildings with its granite foundation, red pressed brick, and slate roof. There were 1289 square feet in the structure, built at a cost of $2900.

Some of the troops on a practice march, preparing a beverage to quench their thirst after a long day.

CHAPTER II

Although the amendment to establish a military post in Spokane had passed the House of Representatives early in 1895, some Senators were apprehensive about the effect the new post would have on military establishments in their own states. They feared the closing of a post or a serious reduction in personnel. Bitter opposition initially came from Congressmen in Montana, Idaho, and Oregon. Senator John. H. Mitchell of Oregon finally conceded to the amendment which declared that there was no intention to abandon Fort Vancouver in Washington, just across the Columbia River from Portland, Oregon. However, military officials did schedule posts near Spokane, including Fort Spokane at the confluence of the Spokane and Columbia Rivers, to be closed. Transportation costs to this isolated post were high and the barracks had serious defects. Over the protests of Idaho Senator Fred T. Dubois, the troops at Fort Sherman in Coeur d'Alene also transferred to the new Spokane post and Fort Sherman closed. Flooding was often a problem at the Idaho city. The Walla Walla Commercial Club foresaw the end of Fort Walla Walla in that city and derided the government's plans for Fort Wright as a military reservation.[17]

While the debate about the fort closures raged in Congress, troops at these posts wondered about new assignments. One soldier at Fort Sherman, obviously fed up with the West wrote:

> To move or not to move . . . Nine years in this out-of-the-way pine-clad and flood-threatened section entitles the regiment (4th infantry) to the consideration of the powers that be. Twenty six years service west of the Missouri, except one year where the regiment was engaged in hunting moonshiners in Kentucky, marching, fighting Indians, building new posts or recruiting old ones, acting as advance guard to the Pacific railroad, opening up new lands for settlers and journeying to and fro within the limits of the largest departments in the Army, ought certainly to entitle the regiment to an Eastern station.[18]

Army authorities abandoned the nearby posts by June 1, 1899 and turned one of them, Fort Spokane, over to the Department of the Interior. It was the duty of Captain Joseph B. Batchelor, then commander of Fort Wright, to inspect the outlying posts and condemn the property as unserviceable for War Department needs. Batchelor had all useful material shipped to the Spokane post. That same year, the remaining structures of Fort Spokane became a boarding school for Indian children, managed by the Colville Indian Agency.[19]

With the earnest approval of the War Department, the Assistant Secretary stated that there was sufficient money to begin work on the Spokane post, even though Congress made no appropriation that year (1895). It was necessary to transfer 1022 acres from the city to the War Department after Congressional action took place. But, transferring the donated and exchanged property was easier said that done. Property owners lived in cities and towns across the United States. Officials discovered that one owner of Twickenham land resided in South America; another, in England. To clear title to the various lots, city workers conducted title searches, made out deeds, and exchanged certificates of trust, all by voluminous correspondence with the landowners. By the end of March, 1895 all but two individuals with Twickenham land had made arrangements to convey their property to escrow for the Army post.[20]

By mid-April, 1895, the cash subscriptions had been collected and a surplus of $2500 acquired. Assessments valued the property at the fort site at $5000 for a 50-foot lot. The aggregate 1022 acres and its monetary value were a gift from the people of Spokane. Although officials anticipated that the site would not be given to the War Department before July 1, 1895, it was October, 1895 when the Army officially accepted the deed to the land. Preparation of the abstract of title was time consuming; it consisted of over 400 typewritten pages.[21]

Expected acceptance of the site triggered action to develop plans for the new military installation. To speed up the process, Spokane officials sent samples of materials to the Quartermaster General's Office in Washington, D.C. They forwarded brick, lime, granite, and sandstone to him as well as prices for all building materials and labor. Although cream-colored brick was his original choice, the Quartermaster General selected red pressed brick and granite for the post's buildings, both being available in the Spokane area. It was the policy of the federal government to use native materials as much as possible, the brick in this case being fabricated in the Hangman Creek area and granite coming from nearby quarries. Slate roofs topped the buildings. Army officials also requested estimates for an iron and steel bridge across the Spokane River.

Spokane was not the only community jubilant about the Army post. Residents of the Palouse Country to the south of Spokane expected to supply several thousand military personnel with eggs, butter, vegetables, chickens, and hog products. Citizens of nearby Medical Lake recognized that Army personnel often spent money lavishly and viewed life to be "lived for all there is in it." The attraction of boat rides on the lake, or a swim in the lake's "magic waters" would entice many to their town. Regional residents also benefitted from various Army contracts. A lucrative one provided the fort with the wood for its winter fuel supply.[22]

Strictly utilitarian, this building housed the kitchen and mess hall, serving such programs as the CCC, CMTC, and other units stationed at the base.

These NCO residences, constructed in 1933 at a cost of $13,349 each, flank the 1899 NCO residences and are three times larger than the earlier ones.

This machine gun target house was built by troops of the 4th Infantry in 1935 from all salvaged materials.

CHAPTER III

Army regulations in the decades previous to the 1890s assigned ten companies to a regiment. This number then changed to eight companies with the men of Company K and Company I transferred to other commands and their officers retained for other duty. Very often these officers moved to companies within the regiment where the assigned officers were to be absent for a considerable period of time or where such men were on detached duty. These latter officers then received appointments to the skeletonized I and K Companies. By 1896, it appeared that the War Department intended to fill up the "paper" companies, K and I, and to add two more companies to each regiment. The purpose of this change was to give a three battalion formation (four companies to a battalion) which met with approved tactics of then-current military science. This new policy brought a large number of recruits to the Infantry, increasing personnel from 25,000 to 30,000 men. Although maintenance costs of this increase would rise six per cent, the Secretary of War believed that there would be a 20 percent increase in efficiency. Thus, in constructing a new Army post, it was necessary to make provisions for the total number of expected individuals to be garrisoned there, and their equipment, supplies, and materials. Residents of Spokane and some Army personnel already anticipated that the Spokane post would be a twelve company post.[23]

The Administration Building, completed in November, 1898, was retained by the Holy Names Sisters when they sold Fort Wright to the Japanese. It is used as a Music School.

Captain William H. Miller, formerly Quartermaster at Fort Riley, Kansas, who later became Construction Superintendent for the Spokane post, was primarily responsible for the refinement of plans for the site. With the Congressional appropriation for $100,000 in construction funds approved in June, 1896, Miller, in August, opened an office in the "Trader's Block" on Riverside Avenue in Spokane where he was assisted by R.L. Woolsey, his Chief Clerk, A.E. Johnson, the Superintendent of Construction, and his assistant, L.W. Tolman. Military officials originally planned forty-four structures for Fort Wright. These were to be: six double barracks, 14 houses for company officers, four houses for field officers, one bachelors' quarters, the commanding officer's residence, an administration building, band quarters, a guard house, four NCO houses, a hospital steward's house, a hospital, drill hall, a canteen or post exchange, fuel shed, a bakery, commissary storehouse, the Quartermaster's warehouse, a Quartermaster's shop, stables, and a chapel.

Miller arranged the structures so that future additions could be made without marring the symmetry of the design, a distinct advantage over the quadrangle prevalent in much of the Army's previous planning. The barracks, placed on the arc of a circle, faced the center of the parade ground. Between the barracks building at the easterly end of the hand-bell shaped configuration of the post, the parade ground measured 1700 feet across. This provided adequate space for 12 companies to march in dress parade as well as permitting room for battalions and companies to go through their paces. Miller carefully located the buildings with regard to prevailing winds and to the physical characteristics of the site, using the bluffs and groves of trees for needed protection. As the *Army and Navy Journal* proclaimed, "the plan of this new post is absolutely unique, unlike anything heard of before." Working with Miller was Otto Weile who relinquished his position as Spokane City Engineer in order to do the engineering work at the fort.[24]

Weile made precise topographic maps of the site which fronted along the Spokane River for approximately five miles. The plans for grading the site included consideration of several benches below the plateau on which the post was to be built, a profusion of pine trees, and springs in several upper areas of the property. Although the Spokane River flowed the year around, its water was not planned for domestic purposes at the fort, but rather for fire fighting, flushing tanks, and for irrigation.[25]

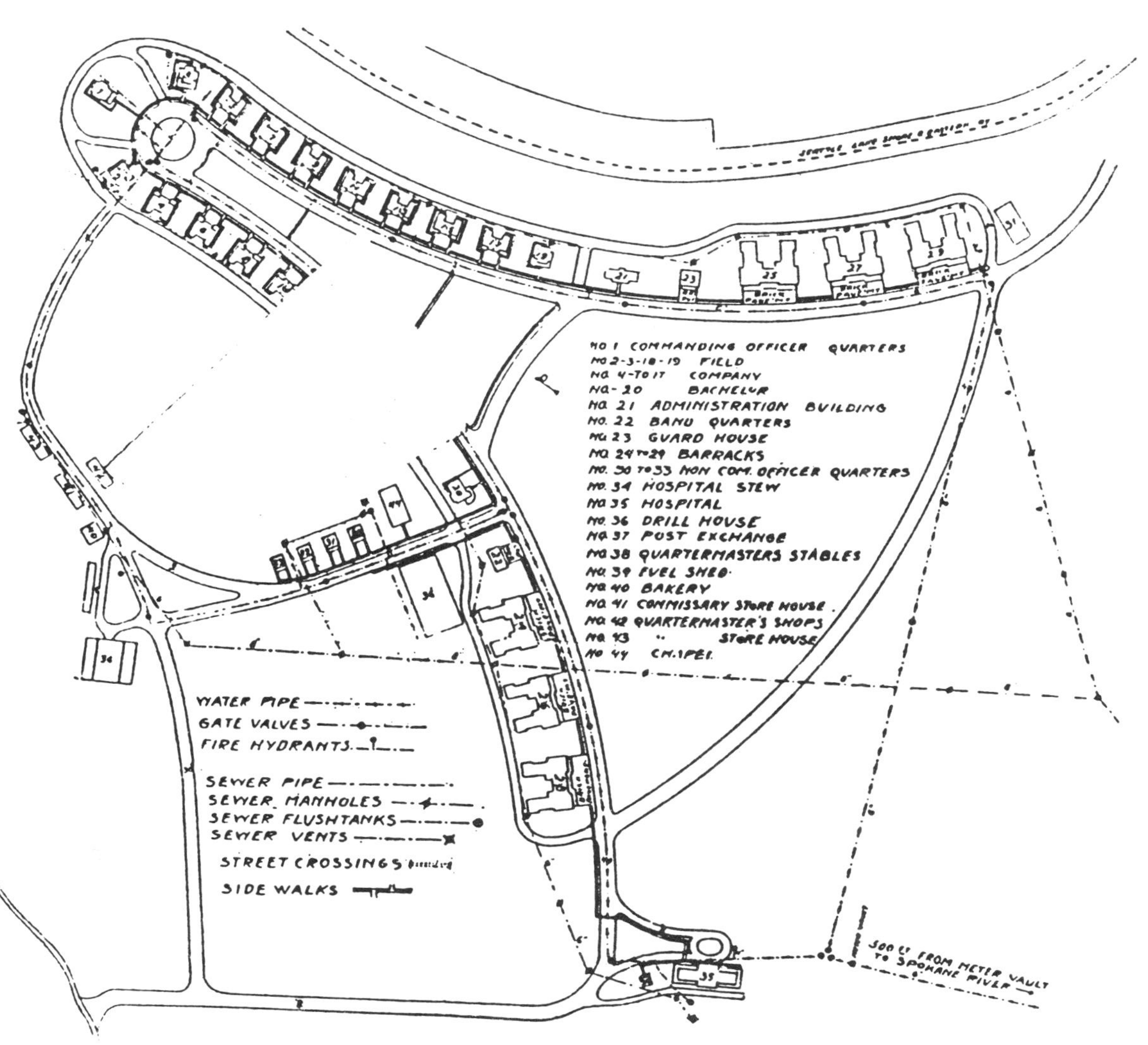

Sketch of the proposed "new Fort Spokane," showing placement of buildings at the former Twickenham site. Copied from a sketch in the December 31, 1896 issue of the Spokane Daily Chronicle.

Two sets of double barracks lined the parade ground. Those bordering the bluff above the Spokane River were demolished. This photograph shows one of the two no longer standing at the former post.

CHAPTER IV

Actual construction of the post began with the selection of a contractor. Of the twenty-five bids opened in February, 1897, nine came from Spokane. Moses P. Keefe of Omaha, Nebraska, chosen by the authorities, submitted the lowest bid — $94,300 — on an "all or nothing" basis. Then about 40 years old, Keefe had been awarded many government contracts over an 18-year period. He had worked on Forts Crook (Nebraska), Russell (Wyoming), Logan (Utah), Douglas (Colorado), Harrison (Montana), and Old Fort Laramie, then abandoned. He also built schools, churches and public buildings. In preparation for the construction of Fort Wright, which was to begin about April 1, 1897, Keefe shipped two freight cars of machinery to Spokane and erected a boarding house and other necessary buildings for his men.[26]

The War Department approved plans for the post by the end of December, 1896. According to Keefe, the War Department had "one set of plans for buildings in the south and another set for buildings in the north." Actually, the Quartermaster General's Office selected the design components for each post, giving some uniformity to the architecture, while detail features provided a degree of individuality. The Quartermaster's office in Spokane made refinements to the construction plans for Fort Wright. The barracks, costing about $40,000 of the total $100,000 appropriation, used as a model, the buildings recently completed at Jefferson Barracks, Missouri. These had a full double front with two rear extensions, separated by a court, thus permitting maximum light and air into the building.[27]

Work started at the site in the spring of 1897 but when Quartermaster General George H. Weeks inspected the location at the end of June, he was not satisfied that Keefe was progressing as rapidly as possible. The problem seemed to be that Keefe was unwilling to pay the charges asked by local suppliers who, allegedly, had raised their prices and refused to bargain with him. Keefe slowed his work, hoping that the businessmen would drop their costs. This did not happen. General Weeks, nonetheless, suspended Keefe's contract and placed Captain William H. Miller in charge of the entire construction project. In the meantime, work on Fort Harrison in Montana, for which Keefe also had the contract, proceeded smoothly and caused some nervous moments as Spokane wondered about the possible cancellation of the post at its doorstep, in favor of Fort Harrison in Helena.[28]

Before construction could begin on the buildings, much preliminary work had to be completed. Bids went out for grading and for the water and sewer systems. The city also had to extend its water mains to the post. Two Spokane men, John Degnin and John Kitto, received the contract for grading the property, including the parade ground, roadways, and sidewalks. For the latter, several different patterns of brick were used. Workers moved over 51,000 cubic yards of earth at the Twickenham site, costing 18 cents per yard to excavate. The contractor hired twenty teams of horses and thirty men to do the job.[29]

Fifty men started the same day to work on sewer construction. Frederick Youngren of Minneapolis received this contract. Costs for the project came to $5409.77. The necessary pipe came from Chicago. The Union Pacific Railroad, which the federal government had aided when the railroad was under construction some decades earlier, gave the Army free transportation for freight of this nature. The Northern Pacific Railway was not so benevolent but charged the government a low rate. The contract for the water system, costing $2757.50, went to James C. Broad of Spokane. The contractor purchased the pipe in Portland, Oregon.[30]

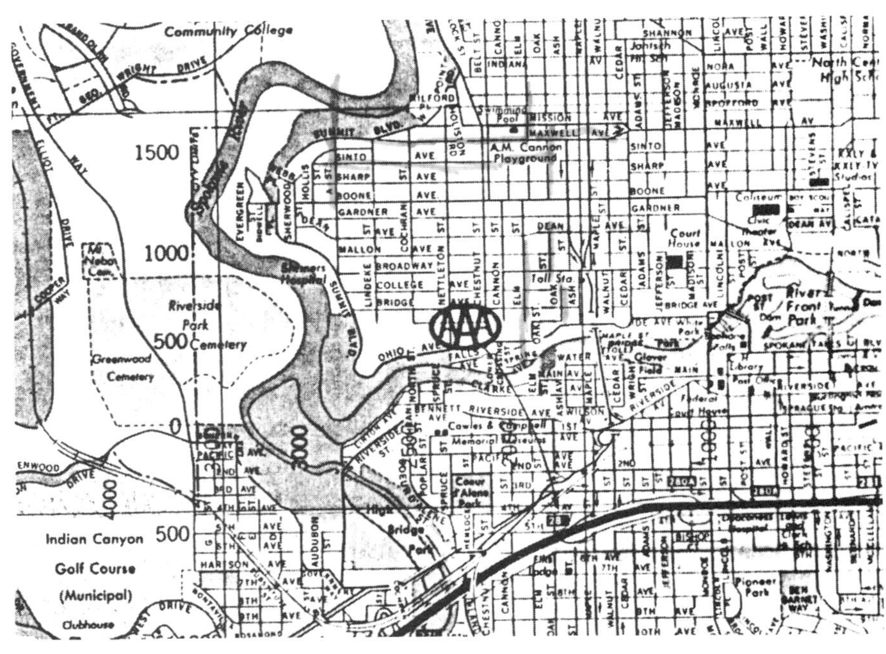

Map showing route of sewers.

While these efforts were in progress, the City of Spokane was busy, for it had to determine the route of the water main extension and put pipe in the ground. Six inch pipe already came to the intersection of Oak and Sinto, and a main ran west on Summit Avenue to Elm Street. To hook up with the extension that went from Oak north to Maxwell and then west to Elm where the six-inch extension from Summit terminated, city crews laid almost 5000 feet of the six-inch water pipe. From the convergence of these two mains, workmen placed eight-inch pipe west to Maxwell near its junction with "A" Street. There the water main turned northerly and crossed the Spokane River on a bridge about 200 feet from the eastern end of Natatorium Park, an early day amusement park. The three truss bridge near that location rested on three piers, about seven feet above the high water mark. Two of the trusses saw use previously on the old Howard Street bridge which, with the third shorter truss, totalled a 200-foot span over the river near the post. Although the bridge measured ten feet in width, only pedestrians used it; officials permitted no vehicles on it.[31]

Before completion of the bridge, an enterprising brick mason working at the construciton site established a ferry which took scores of daily sight-seers across the river for a closer view of the progress of the fort. A round-trip fare of 10 cents brought him a tidy profit for his efforts. But sight-seeing diminished to a trickle in the spring of 1899 when Captain Joseph B. Batchelor commanded the post. He did not welcome visitors and prohibited bicycle traffic.[32]

Keefe had his contract returned to him early in August, 1897, following his earlier suspension. However, he did not complete his work at the Spokane post. Terms of his contract called for completion by November 1, 1897 but there was no penalty provision in case work did not finish by that date. The War Department subsequently notified the contractor and the bondsmen that the government would continue construction of the fort. This lack of performance did not end Keefe's association with the War Department. Just after the turn of the century Keefe returned to Fort D.A. Russell near Cheyenne, Wyoming for the construction of several buildings there.[33]

A railroad spur onto the post enabled supplies and material to be shipped directly to the site without breaking bulk or without trans-shipment. The St. Paul, Minneapolis, and Manitoba Railroad Company received an easement for a right-of-way through the military reservation on March 3, 1897. The Great Northern Railway Company received a license to construct and maintain a spur track of about 1500 feet on May 29, 1897. This access

A railroad spur brought goods and supplies directly to the ordnance warehouses for unloading. The Great Northern Railway received its construction license to build the track in May, 1897.

provided for more efficiency in the construction process and afterwards for bringing supplies to the post.[34]

N.B. Rundle submitted a low bid of $71,200 — about $4000 lower than the government estimates — to construct buildings for the post's operation and received the contract in June, 1897. He had nearly 400 men working at the site and at the brick yard, owned by J.T. Davie, in the Hangman Creek area. Stone quarries supplying the post with materials were located at Medical Lake, the Little Spokane River area, Milan, and east of Spokane.[35]

Plans called for the erection of the following structures during this phase of building: the administration building, guardhouse, bakery, hospital, coal shed, powder magazine, and the Quartermaster's workshops. The latter three buildings clustered in one area while the barracks, officers' quarters, and the administration building parallelled the plateau's bluffs overlooking the river. Officials expected all of these buildings, equipped with gas piping, plumbing, steam heat, and hot water to be completed by the end of May, 1898. Actual completion dates for the buildings varied over a period of several months.[36]

Another contractor, George McKenzie, held an $18,000 contract for the hospital steward's residence, the Quartermaster's stables, and the Quartermaster's office and warehouse. He completed the latter at the end of

May, 1898 but it was January, 1899 before the hospital was available for use. A former member of the Oregon Legislature, E.N. Thompson of Portland, negotiated a contract on behalf of the Bridal Veil Lumber Company to supply some 35,000 feet of fir for the buildings at Fort Wright.[37]

In the first phase of housing construction, Congress earmarked $100,000 for seven buildings: four double sets of officers' quarters (at a cost of about $13,500 each), two sets of non-commissioned officers' duplexes, at less than $3300 each, and one two-company barracks, costing about $38,000, housing 125-150 men. Because of Keefe's low bid, it was possible to build two NCO residences instead of one as originally planned. Some individuals estimated that an expenditure of over a million dollars would be required to completely equip the post.

The Army accepted the water system and the sewer system, planned for a 12-company post, in December, 1897, the latter being "so designed as to perfectly drain the entire post and all the buildings. Having a steep fall to the river its efficiency is assured." Nonetheless, the barracks were not ready for occupancy in the fall of 1898, and the troops that expected to be transferred to Spokane from Fort Spokane apparently remained there through the winter.

Among the first structures built at the post were two NCO duplexes. Each side has 821 square feet of living space. Constructed in 1899, they cost $3285 per building to erect.

All involved in the fort project hoped that the buildings to house the two companies and their officers would be completed by February, 1899 but delays moved the date to March 31st.[38]

By that time, plans for access to the fort from the city had been completed. Although a road existed on the south side of the Spokane River, Captain W.H. Miller, then Construction Superintendent, decided a more attractive approach to the fort was desirable. A bridge near Natatorium Park would lead to a winding road through several prettily wooded terraces below the plateau on which the post was situated and would make a remarkably beautiful approach. Once at the post, the roadways would provide a lovely evening drive for Spokane's citizens and offer the possibility of viewing a dress parade as a special treat.

It was less than ten years later that complaints began to be heard about this roundabout road to the fort, coupled with pleas for the construction of a bridge to give direct passage to the post. Businessmen advanced as important considerations the time-saving advantage of a direct line to Fort Wright and a more easily mounted grade to the plateau. Even trolley car service was hinted as the *Spokesman-Review* called for a united effort on the part of the people of Spokane to obtain the bridge.

Major (formerly Captain) Miller, who helped draft the design of the post so as to bring forth the natural beauty of the site, was not present to welcome the first troops to be stationed at Fort Wright. After serving more than two years in Spokane, he was ordered to Washington, D.C. and replaced by Captain Reuben B. Turner of the 6th Infantry. Turner, a New York native, had twelve years of experience in government construction work.

CHAPTER V

Although whispered rumors had it that companies B and E of the 16th Infantry at old Fort Spokane would be the first troops to occupy the new post in Spokane in September, 1897, when soldiers finally arrived in the Spring of 1899, Spokane suffered a momentous shock. Expecting a contingent of heroic soldiers returning from combat in the Philippines around whom "balls and revels" could be focused, Spokane residents instead saw over 100 Black soldiers of Company M, 24th Infantry disembark at the train station, having traveled in a crowded troop train from Camp Douglas in Utah for the previous 48 hours. In its early days the regiment was garrisoned in Texas but in 1896 went to Fort Douglas. That was the first time in its twenty seven years of existence that the regiment was posted "in civilization," so bitter was the feeling and prejudice against Negro soldiers.[39]

The 24th Infantry had served in Cuba during the Spanish-American War, completing a heroic tour of duty. Following their participation in the capture of Fort San Juan and the campaign near Santiago, Cuba, the troops hastened to the camp and hospital at Siboney. There, yellow fever broke out and became epidemic. Over-worked physicians called for volunteers because many of the hospital staff were diagnosed to have the disease. The 24th Infantry, to a man, responded and performed emergency duties as the situation required for forty days and forty nights. Of the 456 men in the unit at Siboney, only 24 did not contract yellow fever. Thirty soldiers died, which demonstrated that colored soldiers were not immune to this tropical disease as many had thought.[40]

Spokane newsmen, "in drawing a picture to convince neighbors and the city itself of its good fortune in receiving these men," emphasized the war record of the soldiers as they rushed stories to their editors. Their war record was note-worthy, serving at a time of increasing violence and hostility toward non-white people, they often completed their assignments with second-rate equipment and "the worst horseflesh in the Army." The men of the 24th and the 25th Infantry were the famed "Buffalo Soldiers" of the Plains Indian wars, along with the 9th and 10th Cavalry. They received that name from the Plains tribes due to the short curly hair of the soldiers which reminded the Indians of that animal they respected and admired — the buffalo.[41]

The composition of the United States Army enlarged and contracted during the 1866-69 period. In July, 1866 it expanded to 45 regiments of Infantry, five of Artillery, and ten of Cavalry. By Spring, 1869, the Army reduced the Infantry by twenty regiments. At this time the 38th and the 41st regiments consolidated to form the 24th Infantry: the earlier 39th and 40th regiments became the 25th Infantry. Since the organization of the units in 1869, the men of the 24th and the 25th Infantry below the rank of Lieutenant were Black. The white commanding officers of these units often fared poorly in the social milieu of the communities to which they were assigned. This, however, did not happen in Spokane where these officers were warmly received. Many white officers refused to be placed in command of the Black soldiers, among them George Armstrong Custer.[42]

Despite the efforts of the Spokane press in 1899 to alter public opinion, it was soon obvious that little could be done to influence the town to continue its support of and interest in the Fort Wright military. Segments of the Spokane community worked feverishly with the War Department to have the Black soldiers placed elsewhere. The 25th Infantry, when stationed in Montana in 1896, had been scheduled for transfer to Vancouver, Washington. When Portland, Oregon officials became aware of the impending move, they tried to prevent it and suggested that the troops go to Fort Sherman and to Fort Spokane. Spokane officials at that time chided their Portland counterparts for their less than enthusiastic acceptance of the soldiers and tried to convince that community that it should be delighted with the Black regiment. Accusations became so heated that nothing was done until troops of the 24th Infantry arrived in Spokane in 1899. "Not in my backyard" has a long history.[43]

In spite of the lack of welcome by the city upon the arrival of the contingent of the 24th Infantry in March, 1899, through the *Spokane Chronicle*, the city grudgingly noted when they departed in mid-September, 1900 for the Philippines that "It is quite within the truth to state that the conduct of these men has been generally exemplary . . . ." For their part, many of the Black soldiers observed that the very obvious prejudice and poor community relations existing in Southern cities were not as prevalant in Spokane.[44]

To illustrate one western community's high regard for the Black troops, when the 25th Infantry, garrisoned at Missoula, Montana, received orders on short notice to depart for assignments in the Spanish-American War, churches delayed their Easter Sunday services so that their members could join others in the town to say good-bye to these soldiers as they left Missoula.[45]

Another example from Salt Lake City testifies to the impact of the colored troops of the era. At the first anniversary of the arrival of the 24th Infantry, the community's primary newspaper published a strong editorial concerning widespread prejudice in relation to the soldiers, and apologized for it. When the 24th was to depart for Cuba during the Spanish-American War, the entire city lined the streets to honor the soldiers. Stores closed and the roadways were decorated with bunting. The National Guard turned out and the Governor and his staff traveled with the 24th to the next town on the railroad line.[46]

Almost a decade passed before Black troops were again stationed at Fort Wright. In 1908 Spokane was a bit more prepared this second time but the city still seemed to have lost interest in the post and its occupants. Having served in the Philippines, the 2nd and 3rd Battalions of the 25th Infantry began their stateside duty at Fort Wright while the 1st Battalion, the regimental band, and headquarters went to Fort Lawton in Seattle. Enterprising soldiers of that portion of the regiment in Spokane formed a minstrel troupe in the fall of 1909

In residence at the time of Theodore Roosevelt's visit to Spokane in 1909, the enlisted men of the 25th Infantry were the second unit of Black soldiers garrisoned at the post. They received orders for duty in the Philippines in 1912.

and soon were in great demand by various Spokane organizations. As their popularity grew, they organized a soldiers' band which also became sought after by Spokane groups. This followed a relatively unsuccessful try by the 3rd Infantry Band to entertain in Spokane — for a fee. Upon the arrival of that Band in the city, the local chapter of the Musicians Union not only protested vehemently but they coerced the Natatorium Park manager into promising that he would not permit the 3rd Infantry Band to play at Nat Park.[47]

Some years later, however, the Fort George Wright Regimental Band had a 10-day engagement at nearby Newman Lake, giving free public concerts before traveling on to play at the Montana State Fair. This musical group had the distinction of being one of the few non-combatant units to wear a red cord with their uniforms, a special Army decoration denoting a citation for their conspicious gallantry in the Mexican War.[48]

During the summer of 1910, the inland Pacific Northwest experienced disastrous fires which burned out of control in sections of western Montana, northern Idaho, and northeastern Washington. No rain had fallen in the mountains since May, making the mat of pine needles and accumulated debris on the forest floor, as well as the trees, exceptionally dry. Dripping pitch from overhead branches added to the fuel potential. Although most forest fires move relatively slowly, this conflagration often raced at 70 m.p.h.

Due to the extensive area affected, on August 8, 1910, President William Howard Taft authorized the use of troops to help fight the spreading forest fires in the mountains of the inland Pacific Northwest. Over twenty companies of the regular Army joined civilian fire fighters to battle the wildfires. Included in this number were Companies "K," "I," "B," "E," "H," "M," "G," and "L" of the 25th Infantry, then garrisoned at Fort George Wright. Red tape caused a delay of a week in the arrival of the Fort Wright troops at the scene. Unfortunately, many of the Black troops of the 25th were from the South and had never before been exposed to mountainous terrain like that of Idaho, Washington, and Montana. Forest officials recognized that not only were they "green as grass" as woodsmen but that there was an inadequate supply of tools with which to equip them.[49]

The Forest Supervisor assigned Company "I" of Fort Wright to patrol the rear of the Placer Canyon fire lines (near Wallace, Idaho), the easiest task he could find for them. A wind shift drove a portion of the raging fire to that location. Not knowing what to do, the rather disorganized Infantrymen returned to Wallace where they assisted in the evacuation of women, children, the elderly, and the disabled from Wallace to Tekoa, Washington, not far from the state line. The Infantrymen also patrolled the streets of Wallace during the evacuation of residents to prevent any looting of the emptied houses.[50]

Company "G" from Fort Wright was on the fire lines near Avery, Idaho. Trapped on a Milwaukee Railroad work train with fire fighters and evacuees, the troops of Company "G" for hours shunted back and forth along an increasingly shortening piece of track, dodging the reaching arms of the flames. When the intensity of the fire diminished, the Infantrymen cleared the fallen timber from the track leading back to Avery where residents gratefully welcomed them. Among the soldiers was an Army Surgeon with medications to treat burn and smoke inhalation cases.[51]

Company "K" of the 25th Infantry fought fires in Glacier National Park and faced the worst fire in the Park. In addition to building roads and trails, the men dug miles and miles of fire guard trenches and did so with much energy. Their work so impressed W.R. Logan, Superintendent of the U.S. Indian Service at the Fort Belknap Agency in Harlem, Montana that he wrote to the Secretary of the Interior, urging commendation and recognition by the War Department for their splendid work. Letters of commendation for services rendered by all the Fort George Wright companies during the wildfires in the Northwest mountains came from W.B. Greeley, District Forester, District No. 1, Forest Service in Missoula, Montana, among others.[52]

When the soldiers of the 25th Infantry transferred from Spokane to Hawaii at the end of 1912, most of the Black population of the city saw off the 492 enlisted men. No Black units were subsequently stationed at Fort George Wright. Not until 1954 did the United States Army officially desegregate military units although the 24th Infantry became integrated in 1951.

The unprepossessing building was headquarters and storeroom for the Civilian Military Training Camp, 1940.

The Lodge at Spokane Falls Community College was originally the Clubhouse for the Polo Club. This photo shows the stables for that organization. Built in 1939, it had stalls for 21 animals.

CHAPTER VI

In physical appearance, western military posts bear considerable resemblance to each other. Modern visitors sometimes believe that they "have been here before." The explanation is that architects and engineers in the Office of the Quartermaster General in Washington, D.C. generated plans for most of the buildings located on Army posts. This agency, in effect the Army's purchasing agent, established standards and specifications for all items bought for Army use. It procured the great variety of equipment, supplies, and clothing needed by the United States Army and then distributed these items to the appropriate locations.

Architectural plans and specifications were a responsibility of the Office of the Quartermaster General where standardization was again expected to generate economy and efficiency wherever the Army located posts. Buildings of the late 19th century and early 20th century posts exhibit a continuity and a consistency, being of uniform proportion and architectural style. Lacking the design flourishes and detail exuberances of the Victorian era, the buildings constructed in this period were rather simple and functional, projecting an unadorned dignity and stability.

One of two possible configurations for Army post fire stations, as designed by the Office of the Quarter Master General.

Frequently, several buildings evolved from one set of plans, be they officers' quarters, barracks, stables, or other post structures. As an example, one set of plans for stables could be developed into 20 or more different configurations by the addition, subtraction, or replacement of different elements of the design. One barracks building plan could provide six different buildings; fire stations came in two varied lay-outs; guard houses in six, and so on. Contractors used several design elements to offer variations among buildings but which, nevertheless, exhibited "a strong continuity in terms of exterior detail, and interior finish, because architectural features were repeated from one design to another. . . ." Even buildings intended for widely differing uses repeated the same architectural details, giving a subtle uniformity to the structures.[53]

Like most United States posts built in the late 19th and early 20th centuries, Fort Wright fell under the influence of Charles McKim, an outstanding architect with the New York firm of McKim, Mead, and White. It was the influential McKim who designed and implemented the transformation of the Washington (D.C.) barracks into the administrative center for the United States Army. The familiar parade ground with red brick revival or neoclassical revival buildings around it became the model for Army post composition. Other influences of the period produced aesthetic considerations for site development including traffic circulation, landscaping, and structure placement. Vistas, too, were important at posts like Fort Wright. The commander's residence, although never built, was planned to have an unobstructed view over the central green and parade ground to the City of Spokane in the distance.

Even though they were newly constructed, the buildings at Fort Wright provided a certain familiarity to the incoming soldiers in 1899. Each half of the barracks building was a complete unit with its own heating system and kitchen, the latter patterned after a large hotel and having an "immense and complete range." Fine porcelain bathtubs were the same as found in officers' homes. Each barracks had a large club or reading room, a gymnasium, and broad verandas, and the "comforts of a hotel."[54]

The duplex residences for officers, a model of military solidarity with red brick exteriors, slate roofs, and white trim, were wired for electricity and piped for gas, duplicating the barracks. The interiors were finished in hardwoods. The extensive basement held coal and wood rooms for the houses as well as the laundry and its built-in tubs. A small entry to the house, enclosed

Among four officers' duplexes constructed in 1899 at a cost of $13,349 each, this one became Durocher House Bed and Breakfast after the Holy Names Sisters closed Fort Wright College in 1982.

by doors, trapped the cold during the winter months. It opened onto a generous foyer whose prominent architectural feature was a graceful stairway giving access to the second floor. The large first floor parlor featured an oak mantel and a tiled fireplace. Separated from that room by pocket doors, the dining room, of equal size, had as its focal point a built-in oak sideboard with beveled glass. It, too, had a tiled fireplace with an oak mantel, and wainscoating. A large kitchen completed the main floor; the Army added a first floor powder room a number of years later. Four bedrooms and a backstairs occupied the second storey while the third floor served as quarters for the household help. Although these bedrooms were smaller, they are still large by today's standards. Major Miller had insisted upon quality fir for flooring in the officers' residences, the hospital and the administration building. Once installed, workers first sandpapered and then scraped the floors with glass until they were the equal of the finest hardwood floors.[55]

The $18,286 hospital, completed early in 1899, could accommodate at least twenty four patients. Proud post officials declared that the walls were soapstone, not kalsomined, and that there was "an absence of corners that could hold microbes." In 1911, P. Strausser and Son received the contract for the four-storey addition to the hospital. This $30,000 structure provided 5000 square feet more floor space which included a hospital ward and quarters for hospital staff. Re-arrangement of the main hospital caused it to be better utilized by patients. The hospital burned to the ground on July 8, 1967.[56]

Plans for the fort placed the storehouse near the 12-company coal shed which was well removed from the parade ground and further shielded by a bank of trees. Captain Miller planned such screening to conceal other necessary but architecturally less appealing buildings on the post. A railroad spur of the Great Northern Railway ran alongside the coal shed, facilitating deliveries.

The military stables housed horses and mules. Some believed that not even a millionaire's racing stable was better built or better fitted. The stable, like the workshop which held the blacksmith's facilities, the paintshop, and the carpenter's shop, was constructed of red brick with a granite foundation, reflecting the style of other structures on the post. A scalehouse, ordered as an addition to the original plans, echoed the appearance of the other buildings.

Intended as a regimental post, Fort Wright never received the needed Congressional appropriations to bring the post to its full complement. Each additional two-company barracks for enlisted men required four duplexes to house the officers of these two companies. Only when the post reached 12-company status was it usually allotted a chapel, residences for field officers, a home for the commanding officer, and a drill hall. Discoveries in 1933 revealed that Congress had approved funds to construct facilities for four battalions (16 companies) at Fort George Wright, but that in 1933 there was not even adequate space there for two battalions. Colonel George Clarke, commander of Fort Wright in the early 1930s, wrote to Army headquarters for permission to construct two NCO duplexes, indicating the location of proposed construction on blue prints of the post. He was astonished when headquarters told him that the Army did not permit buildings to be demolished in order to build new ones. After months of correspondence back and forth, a high ranking official of the Quartermaster General's Office visited Fort Wright and concluded that buildings that were supposed to be at certain sites were never built. War Department investigations revealed that a bill in 1895, sponsored by Wyoming Senator Francis E. Warren, the father-in-law of General Pershing, had provided for a regimental post similar to Fort Wright in Warren's home state. That post is now named the F.E. Warren Air Force

The original hospital, completed early in 1899, had approximately 6300 square feet of floor space. Additions in 1911 almost doubled the size of the structure. The hospital burned in July, 1967.

The stable housed over 80 animals — horses and mules. Most soldiers worked at one time or another to clean and maintain the stables.

Base. In some mysterious way, the Wyoming Senator earmarked for the Wyoming post much of the funding that would have built the additional officers' quarters, NCO accommodations, barracks, and other necessary buildings at Fort Wright for 16 companies.[57]

With only $40,000 appropriated by Congress in 1898 for expenditures at Fort Wright, little major construction could be accomplished. Captain R.B. Turner, the Construction Quartermaster at the time, was able to install platform scales at the new scalehouse, grade around new buildings, and do some trimming so as to make the grade symmetrical around the post. Turner had soldiers plant some 200 shade trees along the roadways and walkways. An attractive one hundred foot flagpole was set in place on the grounds. Shipped from St. Louis, Missouri, the metal pole measured 65 feet from the ground to the cross-tie, and another 35 feet to the top. Supported by cables, it still stands at the site. Duplicating many other posts, near the flagstaff at Fort Wright was a field piece, "about the only piece of heavy ordnance at the average frontier post." This frequently was an old twelve-pounder Napoleon gun.[58]

Post authorities anticipated that the Quartermaster General would soon approve another barracks and officers' quarters, allocating funds from the general appropriations for the Army. By the end of April, 1898, the go-ahead came from the War Department to Captain Turner. Instructions revealed that the new buildings were to be duplicates of those already existing at the site. The barracks would measure 150 feet across the front, but have minor alterations regarding the arrangement of interior rooms. The officers' duplex, to be uniform with the previous four sets, but slightly smaller, was designed to be occupied by lieutenants. The Quartermaster expected completion of the two buildings before the end of 1899. With two two-company barracks, the post would have space for four companies of enlisted men.[59]

The lack of adequate housing at Fort Wright caused consternation among the officers stationed there. Well aware of the ranking-out custom by senior Army personnel, junior officers expected to move to less desirable housing with the arrival of a higher ranking officer and his family. Precisely such a chain reaction occurred involving nine officers when Major F.K. Kernan arrived in January, 1910 and claimed the residence of Captain Stuart.[60]

Originally intended to be named in recognition of the distinguished military career of Lt. General John M. Scofield, by General Orders No. 123 the post at Spokane received its official name — Fort Wright — as had been suggested by William Kohlauff, son of a pioneer Spokane family. Officially named on July 6, 1899 by Secretary of War R.A. Alger, the post honored Colonel George Wright who perished in the wreck of the *Brother Jonathan* on July 30, 1865. Colonel Wright was then enroute to assume duties as commander of the Department of the Columbia. In order to avoid confusion with other posts having the same name, Fort Wright became Fort George Wright in 1908 by General Orders No. 97 of the War Department.[61]

George Wright, after graduating from the United States Military Academy in 1822, saw service in Wisconsin, Missouri, and Kansas. Made a Captain in 1836, Wright fought in the Seminole War until 1844 when he became Brevet Major. Later breveted Lt. Colonel for bravery during the Mexican War, he was promoted to Colonel of the 9th Infantry in 1855 and commanded the northern district of the Department of the Pacific until 1857. Following the defeat of Lt. Colonel Steptoe near Rosalia, Washington Territory by local Indian tribes, Wright received orders to suppress the Indians of the region. His harsh tactics brought the desired results.

When commanding the Department of Oregon, Wright became commander of the Pacific as Brigadier General of Volunteers in 1861. At San Francisco for three years, he was breveted Brigadier General of the United States Army in 1864, a year before his death.

In 1902, the commander of the Department of the Columbia, General George M. Randall, formerly commander of Fort D.A. Russell near Cheyenne, Wyoming, declared that the War Department intended to make the Spokane post capable of accommodating four companies but that the lack of an appropriation continued to delay matters. He proclaimed that, due to the post's proximity to Spokane's railroad center, the post should be enlarged to regimental headquarters and house two battalions (eight companies). Noting that there had been no high ranking commanders there, he observed that this situation resulted in the neglect of the buildings and grounds. This, in turn, caused deterioration and a loss to the government. It was in 1902 that the commander of the post held a rank above Captain.[62]

Evidentally, General Randall was persuasive, for in 1902 officials at the War Department awarded W.L. Nichols of Tacoma, Washington a $54,300 contract to construct several structures at Fort Wright, including a second barracks building, a duplicate of the one then in use. It was to measure 100 feet wide and 150 feet long, of pressed red brick with a granite foundation. Completion of the project was delayed until 1903, due to the scarcity of laborers, especially slaters. Only five men able to install slate roofs worked in

Spokane, and all could not be placed under contract to work on the post.[63]

Cutter and Malmgren, architects in the Exchange Building in Spokane exhibited at their office plans for additional work at Fort George Wright. Specifications called for pressed red brick and gray slate roofs on all of the four new buildings. Bids were let in 1902 for a warehouse, an ordnance storehouse, a residence for a field office, and an officers' duplex. Alfred W. Burrell, of Burrell Brothers, Contractors, who proposed the low bid of $54,406, received the contract.[64]

They constructed one single-family residence in 1904, originally intended as a field officer's home. Plans located the building to the southeast of the site of the commanding officer's proposed home, at the southern end of the hand-bell shaped green, which officers row faced. Costing $15,054, the home was similar in style to the other officers' residences - unpretentious architecturally but roomy, substantial, and well-finished. In 1906, contractors built another single-family home which was thereafter occupied by the commanding officer. It not only had beautiful maple floors but boasted an additional 500 square feet more living space than the other single-family home at Fort Wright. Some years later, the Spokane Chamber of Commerce donated and erected a handsome lamp and standard in the circular plaza between these two single family homes.[65]

One of the two single family residences built on the post. In later years it housed the Fort George Wright Museum. Behind the building and below the bluff flows the Spokane River.

The construction schedule for 1903 included another officers' duplex, at the southern end of the row of double residences. Designed for occupancy by those of the rank of Captain, the home was to be "a commodious and enduring structure without any claims to beauty."[66]

A one-story warehouse mirrored the design of structures of similar use at the fort. The Chief Constructing Quartermaster's Office in Washington, D.C. prepared plans for the Quartermaster's warehouse and the ordnance storehouse, each measuring approximately 50 feet by 100 feet. These buildings were included in the Alfred Burrell contract.

Despite the new construction, Fort Wright still lacked an adequate complement of officers for the four companies of men at the post. Sufficient residences for only eleven officers existed whereas facilities for sixteen officers were needed before the post could be fully staffed with officers for the four companies. Additional duties of post officials reflected this shortage of officers. John C. Byrne, the post's surgeon in 1901, functioned as Post Librarian, Post Treasurer, and also became administrator of the post schools in March of that year.[67]

Each financial investment of whatever amount by the federal government cheered the Spokane community and shored up their anticipation of Fort Wright becoming the largest military post in the West. Almost as if to convince the city, a Spokane newspaper reasoned, "if the War Department adhers to the established policy of concentrating forces in the larger centers, from which they may be quickly moved by rail, it must inevitably result in making Fort Wright one of the largest . . . . " Not only did the commanding officer echo these thoughts but all assumed that a 12-company post was soon to be a reality.[68]

The Spokane Chamber of Commerce supported Fort Wright and its expansion plans in many ways. The Chamber requested appropriations of $30,000 from Congress for officers' quarters and $25,000 for a gymnasium at Fort Wright. Senator A.C. Foster of Washington informed the Chamber in August, 1903 that the Army Provisional Staff seriously considered a post exchange at the fort and the enlargement of the post to garrison a full regiment. The Senator suggested that a bill for a $75,000 appropriation to build a steel bridge across the Spokane River to connect the post with the city would soon be introduced in Congress to eliminate the existing circuitous route to the fort, and to give a more direct access to both locations.

Eventually, the efforts of the Spokane Chamber of Commerce paid off, for the military broke ground early in the Spring of 1904 for a gymnasium and canteen building. The small wooden building serving as a canteen was grossly inadequate for the number of soldiers stationed at the fort. Costing about $30,000, the new gym and canteen structure measured about 60 feet by 80 feet, boasted two storeys, was much more pretentious, and was designed for a regimental post. About $1200 was invested in gymnastic equipment for the soldiers. The hardwood maple floors alone cost $600. Besides the gymnasium which occupied the entire 40 feet by 80 feet rear half of the building, the structure housed offices, a store, the post exchange, a kitchen, a lunchroom, and a billiards room. A traditional military ball celebrated the inaugural use of the gymnasium. Its large open floor made an ideal ballroom on which throngs of fashionably dressed Spokane citizens and military couples danced throughout the evening, beginning a custom of mutually enjoyed social activities at the fort building.[69]

The guardhouse received a $10,000 addition in 1908. Considering that nearly 600 men garrisoned at Fort Wright, there were undoubtedly times when the addition was well used. Payday occasionally saw some minor disorderly

Worthy of a regimental post, the 1905 Post Exchange and Gymnasium had over 4300 square feet of space and was constructed at a cost of a little over $24,000. It has been demolished.

The old wooden canteen building, inadequate for the number of troops stationed at the post, was built in 1900 at a cost of $840. It was destroyed by fire in 1922.

The 1898 guardhouse had space for 24 prisoners. Ten years later available funds permitted expansion of the building.

conduct in town and at the post. However, the post commander required that the troops be on the post at 5:30 p.m., and after standing in a long line to receive their pay envelope little time was left to visit Spokane, and few opportunities existed for misconduct. Regardless, payday, occurring between the 5th and the 10th of the month, produced a holiday spirit. Even the camp cooks participated by putting "extras" on the menu.[70]

Since 1897, when the city extended water mains to the post, the fort had been using water for domestic purposes from the City of Spokane water system. This arrangement was not without problems for the fort was situated on a plateau at an elevation higher than the city. This caused a lack of pressure which was not only less than satisfactory for home use but which was a reoccurring and increasing problem as the fort expanded, this despite the original plans to accommodate a 12-company post. Although water could be taken directly from the Spokane River for non-domestic use, the necessity of raising that water to the level of the plateau still existed. Thus, the Constructing Quartermaster Department received orders to prepare plans and specifications for a large water reservoir and to establish Fort Wright's own water system. Work began early in 1911. To help alleviate some of the basic pressure problems, the plans placed the reservoir about 200 feet higher than the one from which the post had been receiving its 125,000 daily gallons from the city. The Spokane Utilities Commission granted Fort Wright the additional 5000 daily gallons, free, from May through August, bringing the daily total to 125,000 gallons. Officials estimated that the value of the water consumed in 1903 to be $5000. Had the post utilized all it was entitled to, the donation from the City would have been valued at approximately $6800. The new pumping plant was to provide an adequate water supply for irrigation purposes at the post during the warm summer months. Plans also called for a design which would respond to an increase in the garrison strength at Fort Wright, should that occur. Thus, Army personnel implemented plans to sink a 10-inch well, several hundred feet deep, which could fill the 200,000 gallon reservoir then in use.[71]

A serious disagreement between the post and the City developed soon after the first troops arrived. The City, whose population had grown to nearly 37,000 inhabitants by 1899, dumped garbage at a site along the Spokane River less than 1000 yards upriver from Fort Wright. "Filth of every description" dumped daily soon found its way to shallow locations along the river banks of the Army installation. Although the post surgeon, Dr. T.G. Holmes, filed several complaints with the City Health Officer, there was little improvement over several years to correct the situation. Holmes and succeeding post surgeons were greatly concerned about a potential typhoid outbreak.[72]

Lt. Colonel Edward B. Bolton, the commanding officer in 1905, was as impressed with Fort Wright as his predecessor, Major William H. Miller. Bolton wished to make the post one of the most beautiful military establishments in the country. He saw additional water available for irrigation and as a precaution against fire as a means of accomplishing this, and envisioned extensive lawns and trees in abundance on the fort's acreage. The few trees that had been planted had to be hand-watered for the twelve sprinkler heads previously installed watered only the lawn in the plaza in front of the yet-to-be built commander's house.

As well as putting forth an effort to make the fort beautiful, Colonel Bolton saw to many of the practical aspects of its administration. Noting that Spokane was a young, growing city, he foresaw that the future might bring problems with the rifle range along the Spokane River. He therefore suggested that 54 acres northeast along the river be purchased to prevent private owners from enjoining the Army from operating the range at some future date. The Quartermaster recommended an appropriation of $8000 for the purchase of land.[73]

Colonel Bolton also opened up negotiations with the Great Northern Railway to use their steel bridge near the fort to carry city water to the post. The small bridge at Natatorium Park that supported the water mains over the river to Fort Wright had, over the years, experienced damage from logs and other debris in the water. Many expected that the bridge would not last much longer. Post officials had recognized for some time that the post would suffer if the bridge gave way, for it would take the City considerable time to replace the structure and the water mains the bridge took across the river. Unfortunately, the proposed steel bridge that the government was to build, connecting the city and the post, was delayed for an indefinite period. Although Spokane city officials planned to construct a boom to direct logs from impacting the small bridge, the situation seemed to call for both an immediate and a long-term solution.

Plans developed in 1905 to enlarge Fort Wright. The state's Congressional delegation was in frequent contact with the War Department, seeking assurances that appropriations would be forth coming. Early in 1905 the Senate adopted a bill proposed by Senator Francis E. Warren of Wyoming. An appropriation for the construction of and for improvements to military posts in some states amounted to one and one-half million dollars. Of this amount, posts in the West were to receive $500,000. The *Spokesman Review* reported that $95,000 would come to Fort Wright. Many in Spokane interpreted this to mean that the size of the post would double and would become a regimental post, a cherished dream in the city. Four additional companies would be garrisoned there, two new field officers' quarters and new barracks would be required to house these men. The post and the town were overjoyed with this news of expansion for it meant not only jobs for Spokane but also an increase in goods and services, most of which would come from the Spokane area.[74]

Although the duplex residence for lieutenants was then under construction, in the spring of 1905 specific plans for extensive building came to Fort Wright. The city and the post again anticipated that the post would be enlarged to accommodate eight companies. As regimental headquarters, it would also have the regimental band in residence, a prestige plum for many posts. By mid-June officials expected to open bids for the erection of a set of field officers' quarters, two sets of captains' residences, and two double barracks. Despite this construction, the fort would still be lacking adequate officers' homes, being able to house twenty four officers when the new

An imposing and commodius duplex, this double officers' quarters now houses the administrative office of the Mukagawa Fort Wright Center and Institute. It was built in 1906, costing about $28,000.

buildings were ready, but needing housing for thirty two officers for the number of soldiers already stationed there. The field officer's residence was to be built so as to form the apex of a "V" with the other structure placed to the east of it.

Spokane citizens as well as military personnel at Fort Wright must at times have felt as though they were on a yo-yo. Between rumors of closing the post and the encouragement regarding expansion, uncertainty prevailed. Financial problems for the post had surfaced early. In 1900, Representative Joe Cannon, Chairman of the House of Representatives Appropriations Committee, blocked the remainder of the 1898 allocated funding for Fort Wright by declaring that the Spokane post was "just a place where the band played."[75]

Spokane was shocked in 1906 when, less than ten years since its beginning, Secretary of State William Howard Taft commented that Fort Wright may be terminated. Federal sources let it be known that "small posts" were no longer essential to Army plans, despite the Quartermaster General's denial of abandoning Fort Wright. Early in 1912, Secretary of War Stimsom proposed, as an economy measure, the closing of Fort Wright. With the concurrence of the Army Chiefs of Staff, Stimson planned to consolidate smaller posts into larger regional ones, and reduce the Infantry regiments from 49 to eight. American Lake near Tacoma, Washington appeared to be the choice for the site of the Pacific Northwest consolidated post. Senator Miles Pointdexter of Washington, Senator Joseph M. Dixon, Montana, and Representative Robert LaFollette, Wisconsin, successfully opposed the recommendation.[76]

Fort George Wright's existence continued even though it soon became evident that funds to permit expansion of any kind had a slim chance to be allocated. Later, as the Depression of the 1930s descended upon the country, rumors again circulated that Fort Wright might fall victim to one of President Hoover's economy programs. At almost the same time, Hoover's Secretary of State, Patrick Jay Hurley, declared during a Spokane visit, that the post "will eventually house a complete regiment." He continued, "Spokane is fortunate in that Fort George Wright is on the upgrade and not the decline, as a military center." He further stated that a "sizable amount" of land should be purchased between the post and the Seven Mile Range. To this suggestion, civic leader Eric Johnston assured him that "the ground will be acquired." The yo-yo feeling continued.[77]

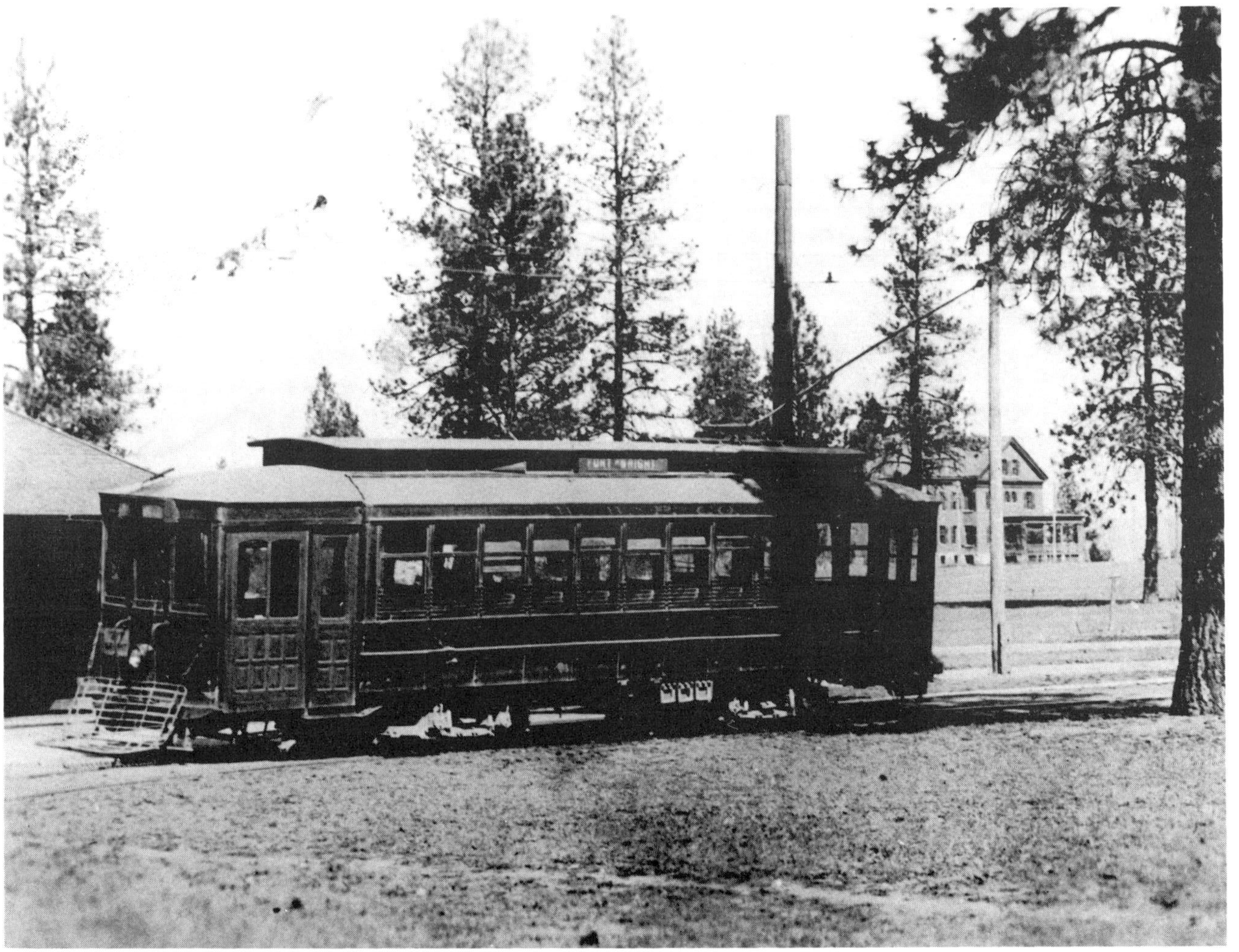

The trolley made regular runs to Fort George Wright, operating until 12:30 A.M. On special occasions, the schedule extended one-half hour later. One of the officers' duplexes is in the background.

CHAPTER VII

Once the basic physical configuration of the post was set and the intensive construction diminished in the early twentieth century, it appeared that the collective energies focused on other aspects of military life. One outlet was the social activities at the fort and in the community. The installation of a telephone system at Fort Wright later in 1906 undoubtedly assisted in the development of elaborate social arrangements. Officers and the socially select in Spokane entertained on a regular basis with teas, balls, informal dinner parties, tennis matches, and a variety of social events that engaged the party-goers in almost breathless succession. As more officers came to the post, the hectic pace seemed to increase. Enlisted men did not have these social opportunities.

Social life at Fort Wright blossomed in 1908, carrying on a tradition of social diversions familiar to the military. The post Social Club, which became active in 1903, held regular bi-monthly dances at the post with the full Regimental Band supplying the music. The Regimental Band was the center of a tug-of-war between the Spokane Chamber of Commerce and its counterpart in Seattle. Military authorities determined that three battalions, the Army Headquarters, and the Regimental Band would be assigned to Fort Lawton in Seattle, to Fort George Wright in Spokane, and to other posts in the Department of the Columbia on a rotating basis. Hosting the Band implied more than having music readily available; it conveyed a certain prestige that was totally absent if the Band were not in residence at the post. Not all the men at Fort Wright looked forward to the Band's stay in Spokane, or believed that the Band should even be there, as an entry in the Post Returns of November, 1906 records. Comments of the writer noted that the 3rd Infantry Band had left Fort Wright for its "proper station, Fort Lawton." On April 11, 1908, the 3rd Infantry Band, consisting of 26 enlisted men, returned again to Spokane, contributing significantly to the gala social season. In later years, the 4th Infantry Band participated in Flag Day observances at the Elks Temple in Spokane, at meetings of the Rotary Club, and at meetings of the Daughers of the American Revolution. The Band also broadcasted a popular music program over Spokane radio station KFPY.[78]

Officers at Fort Wright entertained in full uniform at a "German," a dance featuring a cotillion, which took place in the post's gymnasium. Ladies presided at the favors tables and served a repast at midnight. To make allowances for this special event, the last trolley from the fort, scheduled to leave at 12:30 a.m., left instead at 1:00 a.m. The Washington Water Power Company had received a franchise for an electric streetcar line from the city to the post in March, 1905 and began service in November, 1906, with half-hour departures.[79]

Washington's Birthday Ball, celebrated with enthusiasm, enticed over 100 couples from Spokane to Fort Wright. Many small dinner parties took place prior to the dance which the post's officers enhanced by attending in full uniform. To commemmorate the George Washington Centennial, Fort George Wright troops entered fully into the spirit of the occasion, dressing in Revolutionary War uniforms. They re-enacted Paul Revere's famous ride on the streets of Spokane while Washington's crossing of the Delaware occurred on the Spokane River, well above the falls.[80]

Visiting officials merited special attention by the Army troops. When the President of the United States, Theodore Roosevelt, came to Fort George Wright in September, 1909, the Band of the 14th Cavalry, stationed at Fort Walla Walla, marched overland with eight officers and 150 men to join those assigned to the Spokane Post to honor the President.

The fort often welcomed new commanding officers with an evening reception and dance to which the post's officers invited special guests. The Social Committee attractively decorated the gymnasium in appropriate themes as the seasons changed. Composed of officers and their wives, the Social Committee assumed the responsibility for staging monthly dances. Typical themes, in addition to the formal Washington's Birthday Ball, found attendees dressed in formal attire at the Thanksgiving Dance and at the New Year's Eve masked gala. Halloween, of course, was a costume dance and St. Patrick's Day, a hard times party. Gaiety especially prevailed at the Army Relief Benefit which took the form of a 49er Frontier Party and Jamboree. The Committee transformed the gymnasium into a frontier saloon and gambling emporium. Script, purchased with admission, became legal tender at the gaming tables and wheels, and to buy refreshments.[81]

Fort Wright was the site of frequent afternoon concerts. For the Sunday, April 19, 1908 performance the city placed fourteen extra trolley cars on the Fort Wright line to transport people to the military reservation, maintaining a fifteen minute schedule from the Riverside Avenue departure point. Although each section of the trolley included four cars, people packed the vehicles long

'49 FRONTIER
PARTY and JAMBOUREE
~ at ~

"SILENT BEN" YANCEY'S LIKKER PARLER

Frid. Nite, Jan. 29
1932

DANCIN
GAMES

Refreshmunts

"Shorty"
SCHUYLER
Bouncer

Featuring
"Chaplain" Davis

**"Lambie Dale", "Rowdie McGowan", "Honohula Ann",
"Hum Bru Lum", "Louisiana Lou", "Quack Dokky",
"Singin Hairy Coates", "No-Gal-Is Mary"!**

at ACE BREENE'S BAR

**Check All Shootin Irons and Knives at Door and
Leave Yur Biled Shurts at Hum!**

**"Buzz Wappenstein", "Pop Elson", "Rangor Kid Pettee", "Sharpshooter
Hazeltine", "Moonshine Chrisman", "Rosebud Roberts", "Spendthrift
Marsh"!**   --Cummittee

*Posts throughout the country staged events to benefit the Army Relief Society, an agency
organized by one woman who thought the widows and orphans of Spanish-American soldiers
needed assistance. The scope of the agency has enlarged through the years but still provides for
various needs of Army personnel.*

before leaving the station. Including those who walked from Natatorium Park, and those who arrived in buggies and automobiles, of which the latter numbered about fifty in the city, some 6000-7000 people attended the concert on the post's grounds. They crowded so closely around the musicians that the players eventually had to be roped off from the audience. Crowds as large visited the fort for another concert the following Sunday. Many years later, in 1930, Army Musicians provided free public concerts before the dinner hour at the fort, on Tuesdays and Fridays. The musical programs began in mid-April and continued through the summer.[82]

Newly arrived officers of the 25th Infantry, who had seen service in the Philippines during 1908, had a somewhat novel experience at Fort Wright. They received at their residences fine mahogany furniture to supplement their meager furnishings. A library desk and dining table appeared in October, 1908. Two months later, six dining room side chairs and two arm chairs — to complete the set — arrived. Nine months later, in September, 1909, a library table, two arm chairs, and a kitchen table came to each officer's residence. Just before Christmas, the Army delivered a bookcase and two sets of drawers. Some fourteen months in the future, the government furnishings for the family dwellings ceased with the arrival of two library side chairs. The duplex homes, occupied by officers and their families, received a bonus of a hall tree as part of the last furniture shipment. The duplex quarters for the lieutenants did not fare as well as the other officers, receiving only one library arm chair for each residence in September, 1909. However, in February of the next year, the other arm chair, two side chairs, a chest of drawers, and a hall tree arrived. The Army allotted the Bachelor Officers' Quarters a proportionate share of most of these items on the aforementioned delivery dates.[83]

The furniture at the different Army posts came in different woods. At Fort Wright, it was mahogany. The Quartermaster inventoried every piece of furniture and marked each with the number of the house to which it had been assigned. The Army permitted no changes. Future appropriations allowed the dispersement of Morris chairs and bookcases. Officers especially appreciated these furnishings because their baggage and furniture allowances when moving from one post to another had a limit of 2000 pounds.

The attitude of commanding officers at Fort Wright had a direct affect on social relationships with the community, even though reciprocity invitations from Spokane residents came regularly to the post. Captain Joseph B. Batchelor severely limited access to the fort by non-military personnel while

Captain William C. Wren, commander in 1902, not only encouraged his officers to join in many of Spokane's civic activities but who, himself, helped to plan celebrations in the city. Although Colonel Bolton wished to beautify the grounds of the former Twickenham site, his soldiers could not wander about Spokane out of uniform, even when off-duty, unless they had his special permission. In contrast, Lt. Colonel Charles Penrose, a later commander, expected his officers to entertain and to be entertained, advocating an active social life. He hoped to improve and enhance rapport with the community and heartily welcomed Spokane citizens to the post. Ball games, band concerts, dress parades, and participation in community events constituted some of the activities under his command.

Personnel at Fort Wright volunteered in an experiment testing an anti-typhoid serum in 1909. Typhoid was a dread disease of both the regular Army and the volunteer Army. Orders from Washington, D.C. stated that surgeons would be vaccinated first, followed by hospital officers and nurses. Officialdom asked that privates volunteer last. All were assured that the soreness from the vaccination with the anti-typhoid virus would last only a few hours. Subsequent experience proved that such a mild reaction was the exception. Symptoms of intense nausea and other disablements caused the officers to receive typhoid prophylactics in relays so as not to have all the commissioned officers on the post's sick and disabled list at once.[84]

The next year the War Department made typhoid innoculations available to the Army. In 1910, commanding officers could not order their men to take the serum but they could and did require attendance at weekly lectures about typhoid for all not vaccinated. Nonetheless, response was lukewarm. The result of an experiment at Fort Oglethorpe, Georgia, changed the situation. Brigadier General James Parker on a 21-day practice march permitted innoculated men to drink any water they wanted to imbibe, which they did. No typhoid developed among the soldiers. After being apprised of the experiment, the Secretary of War ordered the entire Army innoculated against typhoid fever.[85]

Every five years, privates under the age of 34 and officers under 45 years of age received vaccinations, except those who had survived typhoid fever. It took several days for the men to recover from what appeared to be a mild form of the disease. The 25th Infantry at Fort Wright, expecting to be assigned to the Panama Canal region sometime during 1912, realized that the vaccination experiment and subsequent orders regarding innoculation had a very practical purpose for them.[86]

An outbreak of measles, small pox, or scarlet fever caused quarantine to be imposed on the affected companies at Fort Wright. When the soldier was diagnosed as having one of these contagious diseases, medical authorities confined him to his quarters and restricted the entire company from contact with others at the fort. Instead of drilling with other companies, the men exercised on the grounds immediately in front of their residence building. Once the medics lifted the quarantine, they thoroughly fumigated the house. With many men confined to quarters due to illness, guard duty, which the entire company drew every eight days, fell to the few men from companies that were not quarantined.

Classes, practices, and disciplinary training comprised regular features of Army life at Fort Wright. New recruits who failed to qualify in their initial target practices received additional training. The Army allocated every soldier 400 rounds of ammunition per year for practice shooting. In 1903, each shot cost 2½ cents. Beginning in the Spring and continuing for four months, troops were at the rifle range daily from early morning onward. Each company devoted about a month to this preliminary practice. The target range was located across the Spokane River, near Downriver Park. During this practice period, Army officials hoisted red flags and posted other danger signals to alert people to the target sessions. Those soldiers showing expertise received instruction in a more advanced course held during the summer.[87]

Fort Wright troops used the 620 acre Seven Miles Target Range for the practice of weapons, ranging from pistols to machine guns. Even Old National Bank employees used the pistol range to perfect their aim in case robberies occurred at any of their branches. Some years later, in the 1930s, Congress allocated $6000 for improvements at the site.[88]

In addition to personal pride, there was a monetary motivation for the troops to improve their shooting skills. During Franklin Delano Roosevelt's administration the Army instituted extra pay for high levels of marksmanship. Soldiers designated "marksman" had $5 per month added to their pay envelope. The next grade, "sharpshooter," received $3 per month extra for the year. Machine gunners also had incentives for quality performances. "Experts" received the extra $5 per month. Even "first-class" gunners were rewarded with an increase of $3 per month. The motivation resulted in a noteworthy proficiency throughout the entire Army.[89]

Spokane's excellent target range made shooting a pleasure. In the 1930s

This proud group of machine gunners, 4th Infantry, improved their aim, practicing at the Seven-Mile Target Range. Top performers received extra money in their pay envelopes for one year.

one class of the 4th Infantry enlisted men had only one soldier out of 262 fail to make the grade of "marksman" and he was only 39/100 off making the grade. That same class had 86 men who scored 306 or more points out of a possible 350 points; 83 men registered from 290 to 306 points.[90]

Sharp-shooting competition was a special favorite of the men. Shooters often used the firing range at Fort George Wright for this purpose because the 1000 yard target range was the only one of that length in the Department of the Columbia and at that time was considered the best in the country. It mattered not what one's rank or position was, for all could compete in the sharpshooting contests. A frequent winner was a company cook from the Washington National Guard which participated with the Fort Wright troops in these events.

Fort Wright played host to the 14th Annual Inland Empire Rifle and Pistol Matches, attracting more than 100 shooters to this competitive sport. Not only did 22 men from the Bremerton, Washington Navy Yard show up, but Clyde Pangborn, who, with Hugh Hendron, participated in the first non-stop flight from Japan in 1931, and Pangborn's wife came as well. Mrs. Pangborn placed high in the second match while her husband finished fourth.[91]

Classes for officers and men took place at Fort Wright between November and March of each year. The officers studied military tactics, maneuvers, administration, small arms firing, and drill regulations. The soldiers practiced daily after mounting the guard. The Army required the men to possess a great variety of skills. Among these were: first aid, field cooking, estimating distance, loading wagons and mules, map reading, and bayonet combat, and additional skills in guard duty, military courtesy, marching, hygiene, calisthenics, wall scaling, tent pitching, signaling, writing messages, scouting, military field engineering, and obedience.

CHAPTER VIII

Instructors at the post also taught subjects found in public schools; most enlisted men could obtain a basic education, if they desired to do so. All the soldiers had access to libraries on the grounds. The federal government provided one of these and the second came through the goodness of Miss Helen Gould, a philanthropist who generously donated libraries to every Army post in the United States and to U.S. posts in the Philippines. Officers who scored above 90 on their class examinations achieved a special status and because of their proficiency did not need to attend additional classes. Non-commissioned officers and selected enlisted men attended courses which included military tactics, drill regulations, guard duty, and similar subjects.[92]

Class work in the field involved practice marches. Each battalion held a four-day preliminary exercise prior to their mid-summer 200 mile trek for maneuvers. In the early years of the Spokane post, the soldiers marched to American Lake, near Tacoma, Washington, taking approximately three weeks for the entourage of soldiers, equipment, and supplies to arrive. Trains returned them to eastern Washington. In 1908, the troops traveled by train to North Yakima, Washington and then marched from there to the summer encampment. Beginning in 1906, the regular Army held its summer maneuvers at American Lake, later known as Fort Lewis. Training at a more centralized location such as Fort Lewis, in the summer or early fall, was an initial result of the Army's consolidation of its widely dispersed installations. In later years, the Washington National Guard joined the Army at the site for military exercises.

Each company at Fort George Wright by turn followed determined routes to specific destinations in the Spokane area for their local hikes of one to four days. Among these locations were Nine Mile Falls, Seven Mile Bridge, Tum Tum, Deer Park, Eloika Lake, Hillyard, Diamond Lake, Chatteroy, Elk and Wandemere. A spot favored in 1930 was Larabee's Lake near Dartford, just north of Spokane off the Inland Empire Highway. Troops also camped at Olsen's Ranch near Mt. Hope, adjacent to the Palouse Highway, and near Montvale Farms. On cold fall nights as the soldier settled down after the day's march, he required four wool blankets, wool socks, and wool undershirts to keep him warm. After the longer hikes and the cold nights, the men were glad to be back to the comforts of their barracks and the routine of post life.

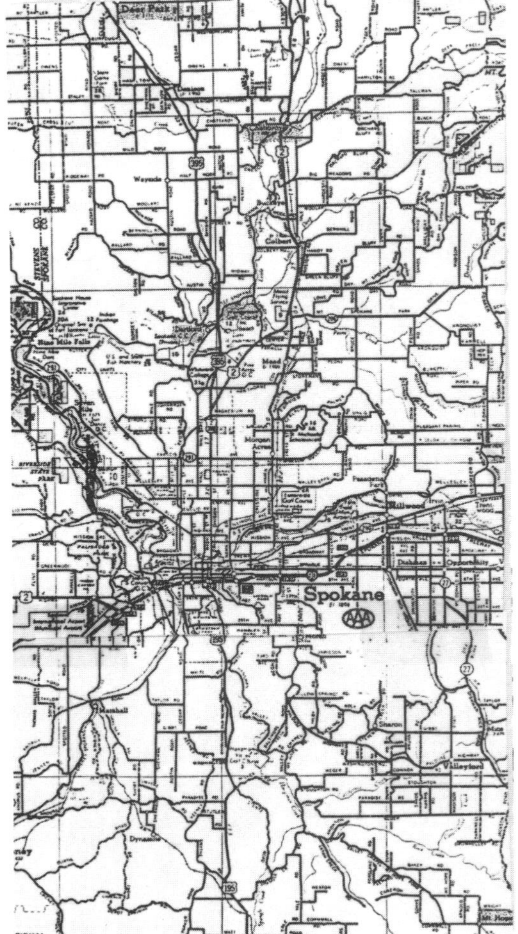

"Practice march destinations."

A welcomed break whether at the post or on practice marches, chow time brought the troops in line ready and eager.

Carts hauling machine guns and the rolling chow wagons, pulled by the post's mules, accompanied the Infantry troops. Civilian teamsters often had charge of the animals. Senior officials among this group, as well as essential repairmen such as plumbers and electricians, were not only employed at Fort Wright but the Army allowed a select few to build and occupy residences there. Some non-military families still occupy these homes at the post.[93]

Following training, the soldiers looked forward to exhibiting their special skills. Officers at another military establishment prepared a proficiency test for the military personnel at Fort Wright. Only the "outsiders" knew what exercises would be faced by each of the eight companies at Fort George Wright. Accuracy in shooting, the time taken to load and advance, and the general action of the soldiers were among the skills considered in grading the different companies. The highest score determined the best drilled company of regulars in the United States Army, an honor sought by the soldiers at Fort Wright.

Contests between battalions stationed at Fort Wright often took place. Post officials set aside the second Tuesday of each month as an athletic field day in which all the soldiers could compete. Additionally, planners arranged for an annual field meet, composed of eleven events: baseball, shot put, 100-yard dash, 200-yard dash, hammer throw, broad jump, potato race, 400-yard run, equipment races, mile relay, and tug-of-war. However, Lt. Colonel Penrose, the commanding officer in 1911, ordered the abandonment of football. Believing that the game was impossible to play without physical injury to the players, he instituted soccer instead, "the milder British past time." Even though the football games used the open method of play and even though the soldiers needed to keep themselves in excellent condition so as to pass the rigid physical examinations of the U.S. Army, the players declared that football was "too severe" for them. Before the baseball competition had been disbanded by officers who refused to excuse players from duty for a scheduled game, the Fort George Wright baseball club competed with teams from local businesses as well as with squads from the post. The 1912 baseball team of the 25th Infantry, then stationed at Fort Wright, played the Spokane Northwestern League team, considered "big-leaguers" by the soldiers.[94]

Needless to say, the troops at the post were not pleased with the elimination of baseball from their activity schedule. The 25th Infantry, in residence at Fort Wright from 1908 to 1912, had, over the years, consistently fielded a note-worthy regimental baseball team, beginning with the encouragement of Colonel Andrew S. Burt when he was assigned to the 25th Infantry in 1892. Baseball was then in its infancy among military men but was rapidly becoming a high point of military 4th of July celebrations. The players had to provide their own uniforms in those days. To allow for the bending and stretching necessary to the game, company tailors made alterations to the canton flannel pants the soldiers wore. A dark blue flannel shirt and barracks shoes, with heels cut off completed the uniform with the addition of soldier-purchased caps. Catchers added finger gloves — not large padded mitts — and throwing gloves to their uniforms. The players also prepared the ball field for their contests and kept it up between games.[95]

Practice games for the real events, which occurred on Sundays and holidays, took place in the evening after retreat sounded. Only those individuals who exhibited the very highest standards of soldierly qualifications could try out for the team. None of the soldiers in those early days even considered being excused from military responsibilities in order to practice or to play a scheduled game. When the contest finished, the soldier also went back to his assigned duty.[96]

To illustrate the dedication of the 25th Infantry to baseball, a not-unusual event for that unit occurred when elements of the regiment in 1903 received orders to proceed to Norfolk, Nebraska from Fort Niobrara in that state. The troops marched to their new assignment. Lt. John N. Stratt, the baseball team manager, "arranged games to be played all along the line of march and the team won every game that it played during its 254 miles of marching."[97]

In addition to favored activities, the soldiers kept busy in a number of ways. Maintaining the post in a neat, orderly fashion was a constant job. An early commander at Fort Wright had his troops clear ground for post gardens, develop land to be used as a cemetery, construct the rifle range, and tap a stream for water. Soldiers in the guard house were assigned the garbage detail, kitchen work, and other less attractive tasks around the post.

The post chaplain established a variety of activities to keep servicemen out of downtown Spokane saloons, dives, and other undesirable enterprises. Among a number of devices, he initiated a post theatre, using the auditorium of the Post Exchange for presentations. The Post Exchange Council approved the use of amusement funds for the construction of a stage, scenery, drop curtains, and other equipment. Almost immediately, the chaplain staged theatrical productions which many at the fort attended. Besides Bible study classes, Chaplain Oscar J.W. Scott promoted a literary society for enlisted men, NCOs, and their families. At weekly gatherings, the group held debates, shared readings, and participated in music programs or athletics.

Through the efforts of Temperance Movement members, the canteen at Army posts across the country, an outgrowth of the British Army experience in India, disappeared. The loss was a significant one. There was nothing at the canteen to degrade or to lower the status of a good, respectable man. The canteen functioned as the enlisted man's club. Even the branch of the YWCA at the post, popular with everyone, did not fill the void. Colonel Penrose, who assumed command in 1911, argued that the re-establishment of the Army Canteen would increase discipline by about 30 percent and be an advantage to the soldier as well. He believed that the men needed a place on the post to go to drink some beer, to play billiards and cards, and other such games. Old soldiers could remember the day when whiskey was part of the regular government ration, making the sale of beer and wine at the post a rather mild enterprise. The presence of the canteen would prevent military men from associating with the "very lowest class of humanity with which society is cursed," stated Colonel Penrose. The tea-totaller recruiting officer also endorsed the institution of the canteen.[98]

When beer was banned from the posts unsavory operations often developed nearby. In the early days of the West, these were called "hog ranches," lean-to type shacks with a couple of barrels of whiskey and a few tin cups to serve customers. Soon enlarged to several rooms, businesses added card tables and games of chance. Before long, bedrooms and prostitutes became features of these establishments. More sophisticated versions of these enterprises developed as the years passed and were found in towns adjacent to Army camps everywhere in the country.

However, local Temperance advocates had, in 1910, exerted considerable effort when they heard of the possibility of the Galland-Burke Brewery of Spokane constructing a frame building on the Fort Wright grounds in which the Army permitted them to sell beer to the soldiers. The commanding officer did not appease the Temprance workers when he informed them that such arrangements were not unusual at posts at which there was no money to build a post exchange or canteen.

Profits from the post canteen were returned to the post to benefit soldiers stationed there. In essence, the post exchange or canteen, was a co-operative business for the military, the various organizations at the post being the stockholders. Each organization held one share for each member of their membership list. The Post Exchange Council, composed of the directors of these various organizations, functioned as a Board of Directors for the canteen and designated an officer to manage its business.

The business of the canteen was general merchandise for the military. Additionally, it offered the serviceman a place to eat, a tailor shop, a shoemaker, a laundry, and a reading room. Reasonable amounts of credit were available — until the next payday. Profits from the canteen provided money for athletics, dances, and similar activities, and dividends to the company fund, usually used for members' general welfare and mess. This situation contrasted to the saloons in town where the main effort was to separate the soldier from as much of his wages as possible, as quickly as possible. Post commanders across the United States observed that desertions rose dramatically with the abolishment of the post canteen.

Access by the soldiers to Natatorium Park, Spokane's well-known amusement center of previous decades, was another matter, however. Because of frequent reports of trouble between enlisted men and civilians at the pedestrian bridge crossing the Spokane River near the post, post officials required enlisted men to take a streetcar from the post to the city and then transfer downtown to reach Nat park, directly across the river from Fort Wright. On orders of Lt. Colonel Penrose, two privates and a non-commissioned officer stood on the Fort Wright side of the bridge to prevent any infractions of the order. Allegedly, it also protected women and children who used the bridge to reach the fort for the three-times-per-week concerts.[99]

Due to reports of difficulties between soldiers and pedestrians at the footbridge over the Spokane River linking the post and Natatorium Park, Lt. Col. Penrose ordered enlisted men to take a streetcar from the post to downtown, transfer to another streetcar and ride out to Nat. Park. He stationed military personnel at the bridge to prevent any infraction of his orders.

Traditionally, it had been the policy of the United States to maintain a rather small peace-time Army. This was reflected in 1913 by the strength of the garrison at Fort George Wright. Due to the lack of re-enlistments and enlistments, as well as to discharges, 425 men, comprising eight companies, were then at the Fort. This was approximately 60 percent of authorization. During 1908, the number of enlisted men fluctuated from a low of 383 (January) to a high of 562 (October), while the number of officers changed little, ranging from 30 to 34.[100]

Peace-time Infantry companies had approximately 65 men while the field service strength would be 108 soldiers. This shortage of manpower concerned some military men, and they believed that the Army was "poorly proportioned with over one-third of the nation's 22,000 Infantry men . . . outside the United States. It is . . . expensive, and insufficient for the purpose for which it was maintained." They saw the then-current situation resulting from political expediency rather that from the needs of national defense. The U.S. Infantry comprised 25 regiments prior to the Spanish-American War, but grew to only 30 regiments as World War I approached. The national defense policy of the time relied on citizen-soldiers, and a small regular army. This, combined with the prevalent rumors of eliminating a large number of Army posts generated grave concern among many military men.[101]

Nonetheless, troops at Fort Wright had a proscribed schedule to meet, winter or summer. During the latter season, reveille sounded at 5:00 a.m., followed by breakfast one-half hour later. Fatigue or stable duty occupied the soldier between 6:00 a.m. and 7:30 a.m. Drill lasted until 10:30 a.m., with Parade coming at 11:00 a.m. Within fifteen minutes the guard was mounted. Dinner tables called the troops at noon; fatigue occupied the period from 1:30 p.m. to 4:30 p.m. The stables then saw soldiers again for thirty minutes. At 5:00 p.m. the troops sat down to supper; retreat came at 5:30 p.m. Taps sounded at 11:00 p.m., two hours after Tattoo. Inspection of the men, their barracks, and their equipment replaced drills on Saturday. The last day of the month the soldiers marched in review before inspection and muster took place.

As World War I drew closer, a number of concerned citizens began to train for the necessary skills of military life. The local Sons of Veterans organization started preliminary instruction in military tactics during the summer of 1916. The first group of volunteers to respond ranged in age from 18 to 54 years. Somewhat later, they drilled in the Armory in Spokane with some 150 men in attendance to whom they issued firearms as part of the training exercises. Eventually, two companies of one hundred men each participated in the training. Those with previous drill experience became non-commissioned officers.[102]

United States action in World War I brought changes to the Army. Not only were new companies, such as supply and machine gun, added to the regiment but new opportunities came to enlisted men. In 1917, the Army encouraged soldiers to take training for officer positions in the new National Army, and also to form the nuclei of new organizations. Many responded to these challenges as privates and non-commissioned officers to become officers and NCOs in the newly created armed forces.[103]

Amicable relationships between Army personnel and Spokane citizens existed by this era, due in large part to previously enlisted men and officers at the post. Nonetheless, in the post World War I period, interest developed in promoting friendships between Spokane and the enlisted men of the regular Army, as contrasted with the friendships between Spokane citizens and officers in previous decades. One of the methods of consolidating friendships involved Spokane citizens organizations "adopting" a unit at Fort Wright. Residents and Army staff scheduled creative events for the two groups. Company "C" of the 21st Infantry then at Fort Wright gave a series of Company dinners during the winter of 1921. Mrs. Nellie A. Bowers, its patroness, and thirty young ladies from Spokane attended one such event. The Company cooks prepared and served an exceptional dinner which, allegedly, would have done credit to a professional caterer. The Company First Sergeant and Mrs. F.A. Noteware, hostess of the post, guided arrangements for the evening. Dancing to the music of the 21st Infantry Band occurred at the home of the hostess. Attendance was strictly limited to members of the unit and to the young ladies invited by Mrs. Noteware.[104]

CHAPTER IX

A commander of the post in the early 1930s, Major George S. Clarke, re-emphasized the contribution of Fort George Wright to the Spokane economy when he declared during the Great Depression that "$550,000 is placed in the channels of trade by the Fort." Some of this amount came from the establishment of the Fort George Wright District of the Civilian Conservation Corps, which had its headquarters at the Fort. The District stretched from Lake Chelan, Washington to Libby, Montana, extending from the Canadian border in the north to a boundary just south of Moscow, Idaho. By the summer of 1933, forty-five companies of two hundred men each worked in camps throughout the region. Materials for the development of these camps, costing $4000 to $5000 each, were purchased in the Inland Empire. During the following four and one-half years, 250 companies formed, with 600 officers and 40,000 men, all under the administration of the Fort George Wright District.[105]

In this aerial view of Fort George Wright, the Hospital and Hospital Steward's quarters are in the lower left. Barracks, guardhouse, administration buildings, and officers' duplexes stretch along the bluff above the Spokane River. Barracks, bachelors' quarters, duplexes are along the street, left center. Photo was taken prior to 1933.

According to an interview with Colonel George Clarke in May, 1964, when first informed to prepare for several thousand individuals in the CCC program at Fort Wright, then commander Colonel Wallace MacNamara refused to act. This was understandable in light of the Army's self-image and in light of the housing problems such a large number of men would create. Then Major Clarke took it upon himself to make the arrangements ordered by Army officials. When Colonel MacNamara saw the encamped CCC men, he had a stroke from which he never recovered.[106]

The Civilian Conservation Corps (CCC) was a well-known federal program, initiated during the Great Depression. With citizenship and employability as its major goals, the program taught participants how to live and work together, and to think in terms of their responsibilities to their community and to the nation, while conserving natural resources.

The educational emphasis at each CCC camp developed around enrollee needs, aptitudes, and interests. Most of the young men had no previous work experience and required training in order to accomplish the project assigned to that particular camp. Vocational classes included a variety of employable skills that ranged from jack hammer operation to blue print reading, cooking, baking, and farm engineering. Leisure time activities were corrolated to the technical service instruction.

At one of the CCC camps a company from Kentucky whose members could neither read nor write learned in one month to write well enough to send letters home. Colonel George Clarke arranged to have Circuit Riders read these letters to the families.[107]

The mountains of the Pacific Northwest were unfamiliar territory for many of the CCC recruits. One company at Lake Chelan did not go out of their barracks for six weeks because they were certain the "bears and Indians would get them."[108]

The CCC District Quartermaster at Fort Wright provided the men with clothing, food, equipment, housing, and transportation during their minimum six-month stay. The Headquarters unit at Fort George Wright was also responsible for purchasing and contracting supplies and services, for construction of the CCC buildings, repair and maintenance, and for the operation and repair of utilities. In addition, Headquarters provided the services of a camp surgeon who inspected the camp daily to ascertain adequate sanitary conditions and the general condition of the camp. He also approved the menus to be served to the enrollees. The CCC furnished dental examinations and care to those who needed them. Two Veterinary officers assigned to the CCC assured that meat and dairy products met specifications. The drinking water at each of the 22 camps came under a monthly inspection.

Costs to feed the members of the CCC in the Inland Empire amounted to over $3100 daily, with most of the food coming from Spokane. This afforded the city an infusion of cash into the local economy during the Depression years. About 150 items accounted for the daily cost, but fresh fruits and vegetables added on extra costs. Summer often saw higher expenses for the food during the Depression period because Fort George Wright hosted summer camp for the Reserve Officers Training Corps, the Civilian Military Training Corps, and often the National Guard, besides the usual complement of troops. During May of 1931 the post Quartermaster purchased $6317 of food locally. He expected to buy three times that much for the following month.[109]

Army regulations carefully prescribed the daily diet of the soldier. His meat portion ranged from a pound and a quarter of fresh beef or mutton, or three-quarters of a pound of fresh pork or bacon, or one pound, six ounces of salt beef. If fish was on the menu, he received 14 ounces of dried fish on his plate or 18 ounces of fresh or pickled fish. The bread ration was also pre-determined and depended on whether it was soft, hard, or cornmeal. The latter came in one and one-quarter pound portions while hard bread (called biscuit) totalled one pound. The soft bread gave the soldier a little more, one pound and two ounces. Should the menu planner decide, the soldier might received that amount in flour, in some sort of a dish.[110]

Army cooks served ample quantities of fresh potatoes, onions, dried peas, rice, or beans. Winter-time saw the addition of canned tomatoes, cabbage, beets, and similar vegetables in the mess hall. One and seven twenty-fifths ounces was the daily roasted coffee allowance for each soldier, sufficient for three pints of strong coffee. Tea could be substituted. "So liberal is the ration that when in barracks . . . it is simply impossible for the enlisted men of any company to consume its authorized allowance . . . " Furthermore, "all rations not used are re-purchased by the post commissary at the first cost to the government, or if a better price can be had from outsiders, and sold to citizens."[111]

One November, along with the items for the Thanksgiving dinner, at which each soldier received 28 ounces of turkey for his holiday dinner, local purchases included: 1000 pounds of coffee, 4060 pounds of beef (from Swift and Company), 1680 pounds of butter, 10,750 pounds of potatoes, 1400 pounds of onions, 1620 dozen eggs, 978 gallons of milk, 2340 pounds of lard (furnished by Carstens Packing Company, which also supplied the sausages). Armour and Company had the ham and bacon contract.[112]

Benefits from the work performed by the Civilian Conservation Corps are still enjoyed today in the former Fort George Wright CCC District. Some of the projects were the basis for long-lasting improvements in the National Forests. State Parks in the Fort George Wright District benefitted as well from CCC work. Although some of the camps were fairly close to towns and villages, others were far into the forests. One location was called "Camp Nowhere," a site to which the very materials to build it had to be placed on rafts and pulled upriver by horses in order to reach the proposed camp site. Other loads for it were brought by pack mules which threaded their way through downed timber, underbrush, over divides, and between forested canyons.

It was mostly Easterners who filled the CCC camps in the Fort George Wright District. Coming from crowded cities where they were counted as unemployed laborers, many had never held an axe or a saw. Nonetheless, they quickly learned how to fight forest fires, build roads, fell and treat timber for telephone poles, and reduce fire hazards in forests; timber blister rust control and the extermination of the white pine beetle were major efforts.

Special occasions brought forth special efforts from the cooks at Fort Wright. Decorative programs such as this Thanksgiving menu was not unusual at these times. The cooks also added "specials" for the table.

Menu

Thanksgiving Dinner
1924

Sweet Pickles   Celery

Roast Turkey   Roast Pork

Cranberry Sauce

Oyster Dressing   Giblet Gravy

Mashed Potatoes   Candied Sweet Potatoes

Creamed Carrots

Hot Buns   Fresh Bread

Butter   Honey

Pumpkin Pie   Mince Pie

Cocoanut Layer Cake

Bananas   Oranges   Grapes   Apples

Coffee   Cocoa

Cigars   Cigarettes

TARGET SUPPLY CO., CHATTANOOGA, TENN

Roster

Headquarters Co., 4th Infantry

Thanksgiving 1924

CAPTAIN B. F. MARTIN
First Lieutenant J. T. Sunstone
First Lieutenant Michael A. Quinn
Master Sergeant Edward Blair
First Sergeant Joseph E. Curtis
Staff Sergeant James G. Mingle
Mess Sergeant Ed H. Hodge
Supply Sergeant Gordon K. Mayhew

SERGEANT
Van Vlymen, James

CORPORALS

Bjordahl, Oscar J.	Johnson, Frank	Lambert, John B.
Early, John W.	Lowe, Oddis L.	Willoughby, Edward C.
White, Clarence	Van Dusen, Paul F.	

PRIVATES—FIRST CLASS

Curtis, Arthur	Hartson, Everett H.	Martin, Sherman F.
Eldred, James A.	Hines, Howard J.	Mitchel, Claude T.
Fifield, Albert C.	Huff, John M.	Tear, Charley J.
Greenlee, Pearl E.	Jagger, Ellis E.	Telin, Matthew 1.
Harris, Benjamin C.	Loper, John J.	Warkins, Norman R.

PRIVATES

Barry, Frank	Huestis, Harry W.	Peacock, John H.
Bowers, Robert T.	Hull, Russell G.	Rogers, James
Conrad, Melvin	Kates, Louis J.	Sage, Arthur W.
Dennis, William S.	Kitrel, Oscar E.	Schwensen, Henry R.
Durham, Galva R.	Martin, Fred D.	Talley, Curtis
Emmett, Frank J.	McIntee, Lawrence W.	Talley, Willie
Erickson, Carl H.	Merino, John	Wright, Roy
Fjone, Hans O.	Parker, Walter L.	Lehinger, John W.
	Proctor, Robert R.	

men flocked to those agencies and programs which offered some stability in their lives. Among these was the C.M.T.C., the Civilian Military Training Corps, the high school equivalent of the R.O.T.C. Many more applicants than could be accommodated eagerly sought places in this program. Coming from eastern Washington and ten counties of northern Idaho, two hundred young men arrived at Fort Wright in June, 1931 for a 30-day C.M.T.C. session. Some estimated that $10,000 would be spent in conjunction with this program, part of which included costs to feed the participants, with provisions again coming from the inland Pacific Northwest.[114]

After a thorough physical examination, the Quartermaster issued the students clothing and other equipment, including the following: two pairs of cotton pants, one service hat, one flannel shirt, one pair of shoes, four pairs of light wool stockings, two cotton shirts, two belts, three blankets, two pillowcases, one coat, one cot, one hat cord, one mattress cover, one black tie, one hat, one mattress, four patches, one pillow, one pair denim trousers, one can of meat, one canteen, one pack carrier, one cup, one each knife, fork, and spoon, one haversack, one pole, tent and shelter, one pouch, one frontside tent cover, one gun sling, one bayonet, one rifle, one scabbard, one first aid pack.[115]

Several summer classes took place simultaneously at the post. Besides the high school C.M.T.C. schedule, ninety college students encamped for six weeks at Fort Wright. Approximately $8000 was spent in Spokane during this training event. There at the same time were some sixty officers of the 385th Infantry Reserve Corps. Coming from all parts of the state, they added another $8000 to Spokane's income during their two-week stay early in the Depression.[116]

The C.M.T.C. training consisted of four levels. Young men, aged 17 to 24, who had never participated in an encampment could enter the basic stage. Their training emphasized bodily development, athletics, drilling, first aid, personal hygiene, camp sanitation, courtesy, and discipline. Returning second year students at camp could be no older than 25 years of age. They continued the instruction in more advanced classes of the previous summer's schedule, and also received infantry instructions.

To advance to the third level, it was necessary for students to have attended the two previous summers, and be between the ages of 18 and 28 years old. The purpose of this specialized course was to bring the C.M.T.C. young men to a point whereby they could train others and also function as non-commissioned officers. The final level prepared the student, no older that 31, to serve as a junior officer at camp. He must have had a high school education, or the equivalent, and have been in the program for the preceding three years. Upon completion of the summer program, he was prepared for candidacy in the Officers Reserve Corps.

The Civilian Military Training Corps was an expansion of a concept by General Leonard Wood who first experimented with the idea in Plattsburg, New York. Stressing coursework in citizenship, patriotism, the importance of military training, self-discipline, and certain physical standards, the General obviously convinced Congress of the value of the program for that body funded the C.M.T.C. from 1921 well into the 1930's.[117]

A variety of recreational facilities were available to those men stationed at the post during the Depression years. Tennis matches on the hard-surfaced courts were popular events. Volleyball and pool games attracted many individuals as players and spectators. Later, the Army installed a Par-3 pitch and putt course and a 9-hole golf course (ranging from 49-111 yards) at the west end of the parade ground. Although the Service Club was the site for several dances each month, in addition to the basketball and boxing matches held there, it was superceded by a new Post Exchange, built in 1938. The new building had bowling alleys and other recreational features.

Tradition and pride in one's unit have long been associated with the military. Military celebrations and parades reflect these qualities, especially for the civilian population. Unfortunately, when the War Department consolidated some units following the Civil War, the heritage of these regiments disappeared. In 1894, Lt. H.W. Hovey brought this situation to the attention of the War Department. To help erase sour memories of some of the regiments, the Department eventually instituted "Regimental Day" in 1922, a day of importance in regimental history. The day selected served as a holiday, commemorated with suitable ceremonies to illuminate the history and traditions of the unit.

Different elements of the military establishment also celebrated "their day." Currently, in Spokane, military forces march in the Armed Forces Day Parade during Lilac Week. In the fall of 1939, Navy and Marine officers came to the city for the annual observance of Navy Day. At that time they witnessed newly instituted Army drill regulations as 600 men of the 4th Infantry passed in review at Fort George Wright. Whereas troops paraded before in single rank, these were now in platoon formation, marching to the

Holiday time saw the Post Exchange, built in 1938, decorated with a Christmas theme. The Holy Names Sisters used the building for administrative offices when they operated a Conference, Education, and Retreat Center on the former post in the mid 1980s.

4th Infantry Band. A part of the formal celebration of Navy Day was an elegant dinner and Navy Day ball. Dining at the nationally famous Davenport Hotel, the party-goers then moved on to the Officers and Civilians Club on the grounds of Fort Wright for dancing and celebrating.[118]

Ominous news from Europe prompted the Army to install sentry posts at both entrances to Fort Wright in the summer of 1941. All persons who wished to come onto the military reservations needed passes for entry. It was obvious that activity at the post was increasing. A tent city blossomed, housing hundreds of men who took six weeks of basic training here before going on to regularly assigned units. A mess hall, designed to serve 150 soldiers, saw over 600 men going through its cafeteria line. With mess kit in hand, soldiers waiting in line extended over a city block as they waited for meals.[119]

Company M of the 24th Infantry originally occupied Fort Wright. However, since 1919, Fort Wright had been home for the 4th Infantry, a most distinguished regiment of the United States Army. Two years after the regiment came into existence, 4th Infantrymen served under Anthony Wayne at Fallen Timbers in 1794, and with Zachary Taylor in the Mexican War. In 1859, it was 4th Infantry troops that seized San Juan Island off the coast of Washington Territory in a dispute with Great Britain. Soldiers also saw service under 4th Infantry commanders Ulysses S. Grant and Phil Sheridan. It was a 4th Infantryman, Master Sergeant G.W. Walters who named a quarter-ton four-wheel drive vehicle he tested at Fort Ord in 1940. The "jeep" became known world-wide. Following World War II, Walters retired to Spokane, That same year, 1940, the 4th Infantry transferred from Fort George Wright to Fort Richardson, Alaska. Fort Wright had housed infantry troops since 1899.[120]

The Fort Wright military installation changed hands in March, 1941, when it became part of the United States Army Air Force as a $4 million dollar airport developed in Spokane. The fort became a sub-post of the Spokane Air Depot which was being constructed at Sunset Airport. The Second Air Force which had resided in Spokane moved to Colorado Springs, Colorado in 1943. During much of World War II Fort Wright was home to the 92nd Wing. In November, 1946, the 15th Air Force moved to the post. By 1949, Fort George Wright became George Wright Air Force Base.[121]

Little known at the time, headquarters of the Second Air Force housed a detachment of counter-intelligence personnel at Fort George Wright, among the first such units assigned to the Army Air Corps. Previously a function of the

Service Command, the mission of the CIC detachment covered Second Air Force Bases and personnel in the western half of the United States, and had as its responsibilities the following:

1. Safeguarding of military information to prevent such information from falling into the possession of enemy agents.

2. Investigation of personnel (civilian and military within the Air Force having access to classified documents.

3. Investigation of accidents, including aircraft accidents, for evidence of sabotage.

4. Conducting air base security surveys.

5. Teaching of key men destined for overseas duty in counter-intelligence methods.

6. Prevention of fires and accidents by ferreting out potential danger spots and evidence of carelessness and bringing such deficiencies to the attention of proper authorities.

7. Co-operation with Military Police and civilian law enforcement agencies in matters affecting the Second Air Force and its personnel.

In the early months of World War II, it was almost unthinkable that anyone would be disloyal to his country but this naivete soon disappeared. Subversive activiy and sabotage increased as time went on.[122]

During World War II, the Army converted Fort Wright to a base hospital for Geiger and later named Fairchild Air Base in Spokane and established a convalescent center on base at the start of 1944. The Center was designed to assist those emotionally and/or physically impaired by the war and to help these wounded to adapt more easily to a normal life. It is interesting to note that as early as 1902 individuals in the War Department envisioned the post as a place where troops, exhaused from campaigns in the tropics, could be sent to recuperate. Officials saw conditions at Fort Wright as conducive to the restoration of health and vigor. By September of 1944, Fort George Wright received assigment to the AAF's youngest command, the Personnel Distribution Command headquarters in Atlantic City, New Jersey. Soldiers, following a recovery period of about six weeks, moved on to Santa Monica, California, one of the central Army Air Force distribution centers in the United States for re-assignment. Starting in 1945, due to the scarcity of housing in Santa Monica, the procedure changed and only those designated as prisoners of war, escapees, and evadees continued to be processed at the California depot.

Authorities then determined general re-assignment from convalescent centers like Fort Wright on the basis of need, health, and distance from home.[123]

Music, in some form, seemed to have been present at Fort Wright since the inception of the post. In the early years, many Spokane residents and Army personnel attended outdoor concerts at the site and to have the Regimental Band garrisoned at the fort was considered to be a feather in the post's hat. The World War II years saw a former mess hall, Building 619, converted to headquarters for the GI Music Conservatory. Instituted on a hobby basis by the 707th Army Air Force Band, the experimental program in music expanded rapidly. Organized at the Pendleton Army Air Base in Oregon in 1943, the 707th Army Air Force Band moved to the Spokane Army Air Field and then to Fort George Wright where band members served as volunteer instructors. At first, a small group visited the hospital wards to demonstrate various instruments as a diversion for patients. Interest was much more than anticipated and the musicians soon outgrew their headquarters building. By 1945, the Music Conservatory became a major convalescent activity with many returning veterans eager for instruction in the basics of music.

Due to the success of the program, band instructors were relieved of other duties at the post. Half of the twenty-eight bandsmen gave lessons as a regular assignment, teaching between 8:00 a.m. and noon each day. Every student had two lessons of one hour duration weekly. Additionally, the instructors scheduled three practices and as much supplemental practice as the pupil could manage. Through the post's Education Department, students could earn high school or college credits in music.[119]

There was a great variety of activities, in addition to music, for convalescents at Fort George Wright in the 1940s. Those physically able could participate in all kinds of athletics and theatricals. Instruction in Fine Arts and Crafts were other options. A Fort Wright farm interested many individuals as did the indoor rifle range. Reconditioning programs took place in the new gymnasium; instruction for Civil Aeronautics Administration certification in another building drew many recuperating soldiers. The airplane engine mechanics trained there were well qualified specialists and eagerly sought by the private sector when they became civilians. To serve as their laboratory, the Army hauled a B-17 Flying Fortress in sections to Fort Wright and re-assembled it there.[125]

With Joe Albi at the helm, the Spokane Athletic Roundtable sponsored a PGA gold tournament at Manito Country Club in 1944. The Roundtable divided the proceeds from this major golfing event, earmarked for the Army Benefit Fund, between Fort George Wright and Baxter General Hospital, now the Veterans' Hospital in Spokane. At Fort Wright, the money bought equipment at the new gym for convalescing soldiers.[126]

To bring the returning veteran back to the reality of stateside life in the 1940s, he not only encountered a contingent of 40 WACS at Fort Wright but officialdom required him to obtain A-ration book coupons for his alloted 15 gallons of gasoline, provided he could furnish the previous owner's book or receipt, the Office of Price Administration (OPA) Ceiling Price Form, and his 1945 license receipt. To further assist in his convalescence, nearby colleges and universities often invited returnees to dances and parties. As one soldier commented, "It's the least we can do for civilian morale."[127]

Rental housing for off-base Fort Wright military personnel became available in 1945. Located north of Sunset Highway in Spokane, the homes were unpretentious but much appreciated, for housing during and immediately after World War II was scarce indeed. Tenants furnished their own coal for heat, their household utensils, and bedding. Those in the first three enlisted grades paid $23.50 monthly for home rental; for officers, costs were $27.50. For those below the rank of Staff Sergeant, the rental came to $14.00 per month. These reduced prices did not apply if the soldier's wife worked outside the home. To assist residents in this housing development, the Spokane Chamber of Commerce campaigned to provide essential kitchen supplies and tableware. Additional help came from the designation of Lindeke Street as a Fort George Wright bus stop to pick up commuters to the base.[128]

CHAPTER X

During the summer of 1946, the Regents of Washington State College in Pullman, Washington made plans for an extension branch of the college, to be located at Fort George Wright. College officials had scheduled classes to begin early in 1947. The College appointed special committees and administrators to develop the structure of the new institution whose minimum enrollment, limited to Freshmen and Sophomores, they pegged at nearly 2000 students. Issues meriting special attention included the teaching staff, maintenance and operation, food service, housing, arrangements with the Army, and student welfare. Assuming that about half of the student population would be housed on the site at Fort Wright, they believed the remainder would find lodging elsewhere in Spokane. Governor Wallgren approved these plans in 1946.[129]

The faculty for the Washington State College extension was to be drawn from Spokane High Schools, the substitute teachers' list, possibly faculty members from Pullman, and, by arrangement, from Eastern Washington State College in Cheney, and from other colleges. The Regents hoped that the Fort Wright Division, as it may have been called, would offer basic courses in as wide a range of subjects as possible. However, no courses would be offered at Fort Wright that were not offered in Pullman.

At the end of 1949, the Board of Regents met with representatives of the Community College Service of Washington State College and with former Spokane Superintendent of Schools, Orville C. Pratt. Washington State College still had the branch at Fort Wright under consideration and now centered its attention on the needs of Spokane relative to "junior colleges and comparable higher education facilities." Officials perceived the California Community College model as being applicable to Spokane, then a rapidly expanding metropolitan area. Not only did they recommend Fort Wright as a site for such facilities but the group expressed the hope of expanding the courses then being made available by the Spokane Center of Community College Service of Washington State College. Dr. Pratt suggested some joint action with the University of Washington. Others in attendance declared that although the site could serve admirably as a day school, its distance from downtown (four and one-half miles) would prohibit use for adult education and as a night school. Discussion continued for some time but without much action.[130]

After the federal government declared Fort George Wright surplus in 1957, its future seemed clouded. The General Services Administration sent a representative to the community to determine how citizens felt about the future of Fort Wright. The message delivered to the GSA official was that the people of Spokane would resent any action that would result in the impairment of the natural beauty of this historic area close to the heart of the city. Spokane residents believed that the property was an asset that belonged to the community.[131]

In the summer of 1960, the Spokane City Council filed an amended application, along with the Washington State University Board of Regents, with the General Services Administration, to set aside some land at Fort Wright for educational purposes. The Regents did not wish to be joint applicants, but at their August, 1960 meeting asked that the "disposal of land be deferred until an investigation could determine just what educational use might be made of the land." The Regents did not wish for the land to be disposed of prematurely. In the Legislative session of the previous year, a bill to investigate the possibility of using Fort Wright land for educational purposes died in the House Rules Committee," . . . a possible reason being the simultaneous consideration of a bill to create a committee to study the entire educational set-up of the State of Washington."[132]

Spokane City Council member Joseph Drumheller, also a Regent of the University of Washington, spoke on behalf of that institution at the September 17, 1960 Washington State University Board of Regents meeting. He expressed the concerns of the University of Washington governing board regarding premature specific action for education beyond the high school level but supported broader considerations that would benefit state-supported higher education. The Washington State University Board of Regents in September, 1960 urged the General Services Administration to set aside Tracts 4, 5, 6, and 7 of the Fort George Wright land for use by higher education and asked that the Washington State College request to delay the disposal of Fort George Wright as surplus property be withdrawn.

Dr. Glenn French, then President of Washington State University, notified the Regents at their November, 1960 meeting that the General Services Administration had not yet granted the Spokane City Council their request to be appointed some of the Fort Wright property. The City of Spokane wanted the remaining uncommitted area of the former post as a historic site, while Washington State University was still interested in a possible future site for a Spokane branch of the University.

CHAPTER XI

The Sisters of the Holy Names (Society of the Names of Jesus and Mary) arrived in Spokane in 1888 to initiate a school for children of the growing community. Just seven years earlier, the Northern Pacific Railway tracks had reached Spokane Falls and in 1883 workers drove in the final spike of the trans-continental line. That same year, 1883 precious ores had been found in the nearby Coeur d'Alene Mountains, attracting thousands of people to the inland Pacific Northwest. These two events combined to lay the foundations of an enlarging population of families as well as entrepreneurs and adventurers. All manner of commercial establishments flourished, as did churches and schools. In response to a call for parochial education by Catholic members of the region, the Holy Names Sisters, a teaching community of religious women, journeyed to Spokane Falls.

Following several years of providing elementary education, in 1907, the SNJM community founded Holy Names Academy for girls of high school age in what is now the Logan neighborhood near Gonzaga University. The school prospered and the Sisters soon created a college, staffed by Holy Names Sisters. In those days, the Catholic educational process was segregated and any young woman desiring an advanced education, and there were not many, enrolled at Holy Names College.

After World War II, Holy Names College expanded beyond any reasonable expectation, as was true of many colleges and universities in that period. The authorities at the College realized that they needed more space if they were to continue and to expand their educational mission. At about that time, the Fort George Wright post was declared surplus to military needs. A variety of buildings stood on the site and could serve as classrooms for the SNJM college. It was ideas, not the physical surroundings, that were at the core of the Holy Names Sisters educational system. Thus, the Sisters applied to the federal government for a portion of the surplus land to house their growing college.

The buildings at Fort Wright had been vacant for a few years when the Spokane members of the Holy Names Sisters came to the former post. Delighted to have received the beautiful site and its lovely old buildings, the Sisters were nonetheless faced with the enormous task of making the buildings habitable and usable for educational purposes. Not only had the buildings

Conference, Education, and Retreat Center, developed a short-term use plan and a marketing plan to facilitate better use of the site. At this time, they also prepared for a brain-storming session by a nucleus Advisory group which was soon to be enlarged to a permanent, larger Advisory Board for Holy Names Center.

During the summer of 1984, the small Advisory group determined that a minimum two-year commitment from the Washington Provincial Administration was needed to produce a Master Plan for the long-term development of the property. By December of that year an expanded Advisory Board was in place and began their work to present a Master Plan for the National Register District at Fort Wright to the governing authorities of the Washington Province of the Holy Names Sisters.

The enormity of the task was soon apparent. Advisory Board members recognized that the project was beyond the capabilities of any of its committees, the Holy Names Center staff, or the Advisory Board collectively. With no pre-conceived ideas regarding the development of the property, the Advisory Board nonetheless was unanimous in its declaration that development had to be of the highest quality. To achieve this goal, the Advisory Board invited firms to bid on a contract to produce a preliminary planning document to solicit development plans for the site.

Selecting the NBBJ Group from Seattle, the Holy Names Center staff and the Advisory Board adopted the suggestion of the NBBJ Project Director to re-direct efforts to the production of a mini-Master Plan. This would result in a Developer's Prospectus, in essence a data base to which developers would respond with development plans for Holy Names Center. The change escalated costs over ten times the charges originally anticipated, funds Holy Names Center did not have. Still determined to have a first-rate publication to reflect the desired top quality development project, the intermediate goal became the $25,000 to continue the planning process for the site.

Immediate response came from the Most Reverend Lawrence Welsh then the Catholic Bishop of the Spokane Diocese. The Fort Wright property is owned by the Sisters of the Holy Names, not the diocese or the Catholic Church. The Washington Province of the Holy Names Sisters duplicated this gift. The Dominican Sisters and the Jesuits of Spokane and the Pacific Northwest each matched the other donations, making possible the continuation of planning for the property. This step in the process clarified goals and potential uses of the property with three priorities emerging: to secure income to support the ministries of the Holy Name Sisters; to care for aging Sisters who had given most of their lives to serving others; and to retain the historical character of the site.

By the autumn of 1985, the Developer's Prospectus was in final stages of completion, and a list of potential developers to whom to send it prepared. Another financial crisis loomed — funds for the publication of the full-color Prospectus, a major marketing tool. Illustrating community support for this regional asset, grants from Old National Bank, the Sahlin Foundation, the Washington Trust Foundation, and the Washington Water Power Company enabled distribution by year's end. More detailed information and specifications about the individual buildings comprised the *Report*, which interested developers requested in order to prepare development plans for the site, and to be considered in the final selection process.

In April, 1986 presentations by the three finalists took place at Fort Wright. The developer selected to be recommended by the Advisory Board to the Washington Province of the Holy Names Sisters proved not only to be well-qualified but also exhibited a sensitivity to quality and to people. His preliminary proposal was well-received by the Holy Names Center staff, the Advisory Board, and by the Holy Names Provincial Administration. The Advisory Board had discharged its responsibilities admirably.

Plans called for retaining the historic core and utilizing the buildings in creative ways. Vacant land would have seen the construction of top quality single family homes built in a Planned Unit Development concept. The builder scheduled some apartments and condominiums at the site as well as nursing care facilities. The over 55 years of age group was expected to be owners and occupants. The future looked exciting. . . .[135]

Unfortunately, a down-turn in the economy in Washington State and heavy financial responsibilities by the developer at a site in the Puget Sound area conspired to side-track the joint venture into which the Sisters and the Bellevue, Washington developer had entered. Adequate funding could not be obtained to finance the project as both the developer and the Sisters desired. This heartbreaking news was most discouraging. The long and persistent efforts to preserve the Fort George Wright Historic District as a community asset and the elimination of the financial drain on the Holy Names Sisters had come so close to fruition.

The future of the former gift of the people of Spokane, an outstanding part of the heritage of the inland Pacific Northwest, was unclear and uncertain. The threat of sale and piece-meal development was an unpleasant reality. One could only hope that the efforts of the soldiers and officers who worked so diligently to make the post not just functional but also beautiful would not have been for naught. Holy Names Center staff, and the energetic volunteer organization — Les Conservateurs — in recent years worked to preserve the distinctive qualities of the site and have made it available for use by the people of the region, a gift from the heart.

The inland Northwest would be poorer, indeed, without Fort George Wright to remind us of a different time in our history, a time when life moved at a slower pace, when sophistication was not so bright and brittle, and when the graciousness of life was more evident. The Victorian atmosphere of Fort George Wright reflects these qualities in its architecture, its quiet streets, expansive lawns, and arching trees, planted so long ago.

As gardeners well know, seeds planted in nurturing soil take time to grow and blossom. Such was the case for Holy Names Center at Fort Wright. Through cooperative efforts, the Center's staff contacted various groups to make them aware of the facilities available for public use. One of these was the Mukogawa High School in Nishinomiya, Japan, an exclusive young women's educational institution. The city of Nishinomiya is one of Spokane's Sister Cities. To assist their students to learn to speak English better and to develop an appreciation of American culture, the school arranged for some of its students to spend a few weeks during the summer in various American communities.

In 1986, the Japanese school officials selected Holy Names Center at Fort Wright as one of the institutions to host almost ninety of its high school students the following summer. Several meetings between Center staff and Japanese officials produced rudimentary guidelines for the two and one-half week summer program. Classes focusing on spoken English, for which the Center hired six English as Second Language teachers, consumed morning hours. Afternoons and weekends emphasized cultural activities ranging from a tour of Grand Coulee Dam to a rodeo at Newport, Washington. Shopping in downtown stores attracted all the young women. Holy Names Center staff recruited approximately 30 Spokane High School girls to serve as Student Assistants for the visitors. These young ladies accompanied the Japanese girls on all cultural outings and most entertained the visiting students in their homes. Tears flowed from the students, staff, and teachers when it came time for departure for many had established close friendships, some of which continue to this day.

As the principal of the Mukogawa Senior High School, Yasufumi Kajiwara, wrote to Celine Steinberger, SNJM, the former Director of Holy Names Center at Fort Wright:

> Everyone was so kind to the students that they were very happy during their stay in Spokane. From the kindness they learned not only English but also something about human nature. All in all the trip was an experience they will never forget.[136]

President Akira Kusaka, Chancellor of the Mukogawa schools, who visited the 1987 program in Spokane, obviously was impressed and pleased with the summer program as well. On June 1, 1990, the Mukogawa School took possession of the Fort George Wright campus, having negotiated for its purchase from the Washington Province of the Sisters of the Holy Names. The fall of 1990 saw the first contingent of Mukogawa students at Fort Wright for a ten week program, focusing on English and American History. For some of the students, the session was their second visit to the campus.

Mukogawa school officials have invested heavily in the restoration of the historic site, and are continuing their efforts to update the campus. Staff members from Nishinomiya as well as some teachers reside in various historic residences at Fort Wright. The campus remains intact and the new owners are making substantial efforts to maintain its historic character, one of the three goals outlined by the Holy Names Sisters when they prioritized their needs during the planning process. Actually, all three goals have been met for proceeds from the sale of the site have enabled the religious community to support their ministries and to better meet the retirement needs of the older Holy Names Sisters.

Although the Mukogawa/Fort Wright Institute retains only a portion of the original 1022 acre post, the historic buildings and the tree-lined streets have come to symbolize another era for Spokane residents and visitors. In the quiet of approaching evening, one can almost see officers and their families relaxing on the wide verandas as dusk gently settles around them or hear the distant neighing of horses and mules at the stables. It is easy to imagine troops in front of the barracks buildings and the flag rising to catch an early breeze atop the pole at the end of the parade ground. The hustle and bustle of incoming and departing soldiers during the early stages of World War II live again in the mind's eye. Music still thrives at the Fort George Wright campus for the Sisters retained the early Administration Building, built in 1897, for the Holy Names Music Center at Fort Wright, a successful institution which counts among its graduates internationally known vocalists.

Today, the continuation of Fort George Wright seems assured, its beauty and history intact.

The original bandstand came from Fort Sherman in Coeur d'Alene, Idaho. The Fort Wright Museum organization had the bandstand taken to a park in Cheney, Washington after the Museum closed in the 1980's

APPENDIX A

BUILDINGS STILL EXISTANT AT FORT GEORGE WRIGHT

NAME	DATE COMPLETED	COST
Clarke/Field Officer	June 30, 1906	$17,755.39
Nellie Garry/Field Officer	June 27, 1904	15,054.93
Weston/Officers (2)	June 30, 1906	27,929.31
Davignon/Officers (2)	June 27, 1904	25,403.40
Dufresne/Officers (2)	October 3, 1899	13,349.65
Cere/Officers (2)	October 3, 1899	13,349.65
Bourget/Officers (2)	October 3, 1899	13,349.65
Regina/Officers (2)	January 2, 1906	19,077.00
Durocher/Officers (2)	October 3, 1899	13,349.65
Bachelor Officers	June 30, 1906	36,757.11
Music/Admnistration	November 29, 1897	10,983.00
Double Barracks	November 28, 1906	66,914.12
Double Barracks	November 28, 1906	66,914.12
Hospital Steward (NCO)	May 31, 1898	2,401.00
NCO Duplex	July 18, 1933	13,223.75
NCO Duplex	July 18, 1933	13,223.75
NCO Duplex	March 10, 1899	3,227.50
NCO Duplex	March 10, 1899	3,285.00
Bakery	November 29, 1908	3,158.00
Quartermaster Office	May 31, 1907	9,580.00
Powder Magazine	November 29, 1898	450.00
Commissary Warehouse	April 15, 1903	10,432.62
Ordnance Warehouse	April 15, 1903	3,515.49
Fire Station	September 1, 1906	2,650.00
Flagstaff	March, 1899	882.00
NCO Quarters	December 15, 1931	794.20
NCO Quarters	November 23, 1922	250.00
Oil House	November 24, 1934	621.32
NCO Duplex	July 8, 1933	13,223.75
NCO Duplex	July 8, 1933	13,223.75
PX Gas Station	December 20, 1937	2,533.00
Polo Club	July 15, 1939	38,725.58

APPENDIX B

Civilian Conservation Corps in the Fort George Wright District were located at:
Seven Mile (along the Spokane River)
Kalispel Bay (Priest Lake)
Big Creek (Prichard, Idaho)
Four Corners (Priest River, Idaho)
Growden (Colville National Forest)
St. Joe River (12 miles above Avery, Idaho)
Veterans (Usk, Washington)
Chatcolet (Heyburn State Park, Idaho)
Experimental Station (Priest River, Idaho)
Marble Creek (St. Joe National Forest)
Sullivan Lake (near Metaline Falls, WA.)
Worley (Idaho)
Wolf Lodge (Idaho)
Libby (Montana)
Devil's Elbow (Prichard, Idaho)
Kalispel Creek (42 miles from Priest River)
Blowdown (near Priest River)
Hayden Creek (Idaho)
Camp Drysdale (Herrick, Idaho)
Avery (Idaho)
Willow Creek (Emida, Idaho)
Coulee Dam (Washington)

APPENDIX C

DONATIONS TO THE CASH FUND FOR THE SPOKANE ARMY POST, 1895

A.G. Avery $20
Avenue Drug Co. $25
Arend and Kenward $25
W.C. Acuff $5
A.H. Hanger $10
L. Allemberg Bros. $5
L.L. Bertoneau $50
W.S. Blalock $2.50
C.E. Bisbee $10
Binkley and Taylor $1,050
Blake and Post $50
Benham and Griffith $100
Samuel Bayles $25
L. Bernheimer $10
H.N. Belt $10
F.R. Bingham $2.50
E.F. Bean $10
H.D. Crow $20
Chicago Clothing Co. . . . $300
J.M. Corbett $10
Comstock and Paterson . . $100
J.W. Considine $50
Austin Corbin (second) $15
J.H. Clay $5
Patrick Clark $50
Cash $2.50
Chicago Market $25
D.C. Corbin $100
Sam Crow $5
D.H. Dwight $25
J.W. Douglas $20
George R. Dodson $25
E.J. Dyer $25
R.T. Dilworth $3
Victor Dessert $500
George R. Doer $20
Dempsie & Co. $25

R. M. Denney $5
F.R. Drake $2.50
Dunn Bros. $5
G.G. Essig $25
Exchange National Bank $1,000
W.G. Estep $25
Thomas Elsom $2.50
D.B. Fotheringham $100
A. Federlam $5
Forster & Wakefield $25
John A. Finch $60
T.M. Foster $5
Eugene Fellowes $5
A. Ganthier $5
P.G. Gough $2.50
Gray, Ewing, & Co. $25
A.E. Gallagher $20
John Graham Co. $100
F.D. Gibbs $10
Galland-Burke Brewing . . $100
Goetz & Baer $50
B.L. Gordon & Co. $50
F.H. Guze $10
C.W. Geib $10
William Hoffman $5
D.H. Huntington $10
Hyde & Happy $50
D.W. Henley $25
H.M. Herman $5
A.M.S. Hilgard $10
R.J. Hurd & Co. $25
A. Halgerson $2.50
Hill Bros. & Co. $50
Holly, Mason, Marks $500
E.J. Hyde $10
G. Hepton $10
W. K. Holmes $5

H.M. Herrin & Co. $50
Henco Brewing $82.10
IXL Clothing Co. $150
Jones & Dillingham $50
Joslyn Music Co. $25
John Johnson $3
Jones, Voorhees & Stephens $50
J. Kenworth $5
W.R. Kelsey $1
Kirkendall & Weiser $50
F. Kizer $10
Chester F. Lee $5
Gaston Laillard $2.50
F.E. Langford $10
Samuel Linden $2.50
Geoge J. Loy $5
LeRoi Mining Co. $100
M. Long $25
M. Morrison $1
Andrew Meyers $3
M.F. Mendenhall $15
C.H. Montgomery $1.50
Charles McNab $25
Watson McGill $20
W.R. Marvin $10
A.W. McMorran $5
J.J. Miller $25
Ben C. Nichols $25
Ben Norman $10
William Nettleton $500
O. K. Stable $25
R.S. Oakley $10
J. T. Omo $25
George S.Palmer $10
G. Pettet $5
Dr. C.S. Penfield $10
W.D. Pequin $25

Horace Palmer $2.50
Pacific Packing Co. $25
T.J. Pedicord $25
R. Lewis Rutter $25
H.M. Richards $10
G.G. Reeder $25
Roberts Bros. $25
Ryan & Newton $25
J.P.M. Richards $10
W.L. Root $15
Seiffert Bros $50
Gus Seiffert $60
E. Schloker $10
E. Stanley $5
A.P. Sawyer $10
M. Seller & Co. $100
M. Sobol $10

Smith & Blanchard $10
E.M. Shaw $25
Spokane Drug Co. $75
Stowell Drug Co. $25
Second Ave. Drug Co $25
R.E. M. Strickland $10
Spokane Ice Co. $25
Schacht & Reardon $20
Sloane-Paine-Richmond . . $100
Skerrett & Donnelly $10
M. & S. Schulein $25
John Sengfelder $10
J.F. Spiger $10
Spo. & Id. Lumber Co. . . . $25
Spo. East Trust Co. $300
R.E.M. Stickland $25
Spokane Gas Co. $100

Drs. Thompson & Coe $50
Traders' Nat. Bank $300
J. Elmer West $5
Herbert Witherspoon $1
J.W. Wentworth $25
White House Dry Goods . $100
Washington Water Power $159
R. Well $100
D.F. Wetzel $50
J. W. Witherop $50
Washington Feed Co. $25
W.W. Witherspoon $10
W.H. Wiscombe $10
L.B. Whitten $100
Yuem Yee $5
Ah Yum $5
San Lee Yist $5

Total Amount $8,720.50

DONATIONS OF PROPERTY TO EXCHANGE FOR LAND AT FORT SITE, 1895.

H.C Ashenfelter — Lot 26, blk. 10, McCabe's add.

George G. Ambs — 18½ acres in sec 30, twp 26 north, r 43.

F. Berg — Lot 10, blk 4, Ridgewood add.

Olive H. Bowen — Lot 4, blk 5, Celesta Park.

P.S. Byrne — Lots 17 and 18, blk 8, Lidgerwood add.

Frank Bracht — Lot 4, blk 13, Union Park.

H.N. Belt — Lots 6 and 7, blk 18, Southeast add to Ross Park.

C.B. Bates — Lots 4 and 5, blk 19, Nettleton's 1st add.

L.L. Bertonneau — Lot 21, blk 2, Nettleton's 1st add.

F. Lewis Clark — Lots 7, 8, and 9, blk 11; lots 10 and 12, blk 12; lots 1, 2, 3, 4, 5, 6, 10, 11, and 12, blk 13; lots 1, 2, 3, 4, 5, and 6, blk 14, all in Nosler's add; lots 1 to 15, inclusive, blk 29, and lots 1, 2, 3, 4, and 5, blk 39, Southeast add. to Ross Park.

Theo. Chamberlain (N.D.) — lot 11 and part of lot 12, blk 34, Chamberlain's add.

W.P. Carlin (N.D.) — Two lots.

City Park Transit Co. — Lots 9, 10, 15 and 16, blk 1, Lidgerwood.

Roberta L. Cornett — all of blk 15, Avondale add.

Comstock & Paterson — Lot 9, blk 2, Lower Crossing add.

M.B. Connelly — Lot 10, blk 16, Sprague Street add.

M.T. Cowley — W½ lot 1, blk 10, Ross Park.

M. B. Dolan — Lot 6, blk F, Queen Anne add.

Mary D. Dwight — Lot 8, blk A, Lidgerwood add.

W. H. Downer — Lot 6, blk 99.

N. Fred Essig — Lots 4, 5, 6, 7, 8, & 9, blk 27, Minnehaha.

Walter France — Lots 13, 14, and 15, blk 19, Bellevue add.

Falls City Land and Improvement Comp. — all its interest in Twickenham, 125 acres, free and unimcumbered (sic).

J.E. Gandy (N.D) — Two lots in King add.

Galland-Burke Brewing Co. — Lots 3 and 4, subdivision blk E, Whiting's add.

Great Eastern Co. — 2 acres, sec 26, twp 26 north, r 42.

F.B. Grinnell (N.D.) — one lot in Hillyard.

Cyrus Happy — Lot 9, blk 23, East Side Syndicate add.

D.T. Ham — Lots 1 and 2 inclusive, in blk 176, East Side Syndicate add.

M.T. Hartson — Sub C of Lot 4, blk 7, Hartson's Highland add.

S. Heath — Lots 6, 7, and 8, blk 28, SE add to Ross Park.

P. Hughes (N.D.) — one lot in Betts' add.

Inland Telegraph and Telephone Co. — Lot 11, blk 30, Union Park add.

C.W. Ide (N.D.) — Lot 6, blk 4, Ide's 3rd add.

Mrs. A.F. Jenison — Lot 11, blk 43, Muzzy's add.

D.P. Jenkins — Lots 3 and 4, blk 29, Central add.

I.S. Kaufman — Lots 4 and 5, blk 18, SE add to Ross Park.

J. Kenworthy — Lot 8, blk 12, Garden Springs add.

John Kern — One acre in sec 2, twp 25, r 43.

G. Koons — NE¼ of Lot 3, blk 4, Endion's add.

George Lauman — Lots 5 and 6, blk 4, Fairview add.

John H. Lamona — Lots 1, 2, and 3, blk 6, and lots 10 and 11, blk 8, Clifton Highland add.

Mary Latham (N.D.) — Lots 22, 23, and 24, blk 1, Lancaster add.

F.M. Lownes (N.D.) — Lot 11, blk 35, twp of Webster.

G.C. Mouat — Lot 4, blk 27, Union Park add.

C.K. Merriam — Lots 10 and 11, blk 4, and lot 4, Merriam add.

F. Mason — Lot 9, blk 52, Lidgerwood add.

William Morse — Lot 1, blk 13, Riverview add.

H.B. Nichols — Lots 1, 2, 3, 4, 5, 6, 15, 16, 17, 18, 19, 20, 21, 22, 23, and 24, blk 21, Bellevue add, 8 full lots.

Northwestern and Hypotheek Bank — SE¼ of SE¼ sec 29, twp 25 n, r 43; lots 10, 11, 12, and 13, blk 8, Dennis & Bradley's add; blks 2, 3, 5, 12, 13, 14, 15, 16, 17, and s½ of blk 24 and blks 25, 26, and 27, lots 3, 4, 5, 6, 7, 8, 10, 11, and 12, blk 28, all in Altu (sic) Vista add.

L.J. Ostroski — Lots 8, 9, 16, and 17, blk 1, Cannondale.

George Odell — Lot 10, blk 15, East End add.

C.S. Penfield — One acre.

William Pettit — one and .08 acres, sec 12, twp 25 n, r 41.

Root and Rutter — Lots 4, 5, and 6, blk 41, Union Park.

W.S. Rogers — Lots 13 and 14, blk 13, Riverton add.

The Racket Store — Lot 3, blk 15, Highland add.

A.W. Strong — Lot 12, blk 17, Fairview add.

Washington Brick and Lime Co. — 40 acres, sec 9, twp 24, n, r 43.

Washington Loan and Investment Co. — Lots 7 and 8, blk 3, Lidgerwood.

Washington and Pacific Investment Co. — Lot 12, blk 40, Chamberlain's add; Lot 5 and part of lot 6, blk 5, Saunders.

L.B. Whitten — Lots 1 and 2, blk 7, Columbia add.

H.L. Wilson — Lots 1, 2, 3, and 4, blk 37, SE add to Ross Park.

A.P. Wolverton — Lots 14, 15, 16, and 17, blk 36, Wolverton & Conlon's add.

B.M. Whitting (N.D.) — Five lots in Whitting's add.

Washington Mill Co. — One lot in blk 10, Ross Park.

G.L. walker (N.D.) — One lot.

Washington Water Power Company — Real estate, assessed valuation $1000 (N.D.).

Great Northern Right of Way Committee — Real estate, assessed valuation $1000 (N.D.).

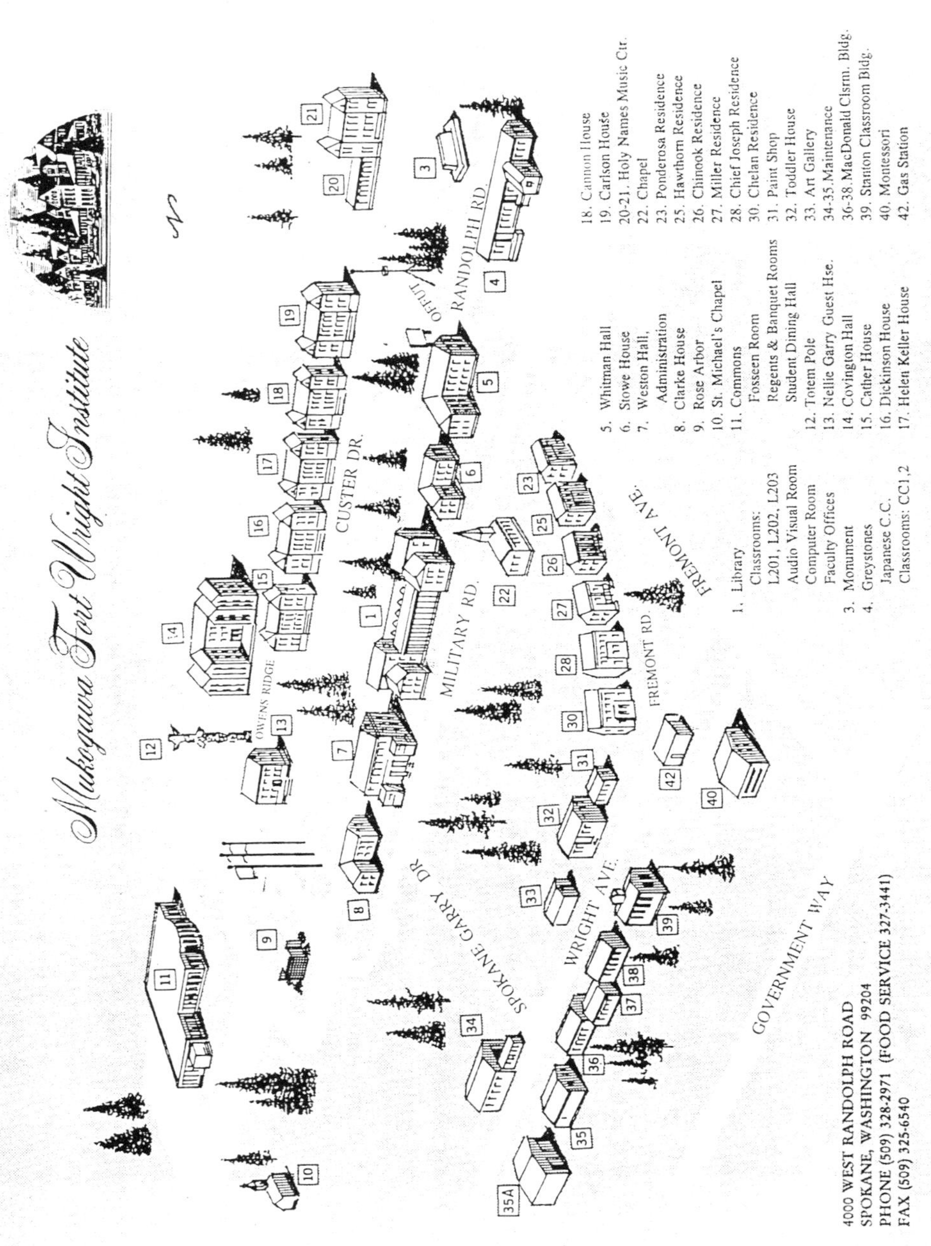

Mukogawa Fort Wright Institute

1. Library
   Classrooms:
   L201, L202, L203
   Audio Visual Room
   Computer Room
   Faculty Offices
3. Monument
4. Greystones
   Japanese C.C.
   Classrooms: CC1,2
5. Whitman Hall
6. Stowe House
7. Weston Hall,
   Administration
8. Clarke House
9. Rose Arbor
10. St. Michael's Chapel
11. Commons
   Fosseen Room
   Regents & Banquet Rooms
   Student Dining Hall
12. Totem Pole
13. Nellie Garry Guest Hse.
14. Covington Hall
15. Cather House
16. Dickinson House
17. Helen Keller House
18. Cannon House
19. Carlson House
20-21. Holy Names Music Ctr.
22. Chapel
23. Ponderosa Residence
25. Hawthorn Residence
26. Chinook Residence
27. Miller Residence
28. Chief Joseph Residence
30. Chelan Residence
31. Paint Shop
32. Toddler House
33. Art Gallery
34-35. Maintenance
36-38. MacDonald Clsrm. Bldg.
39. Stanton Classroom Bldg.
40. Montessori
42. Gas Station

RANDOLPH RD.
OFFUT
CUSTER DR.
MILITARY RD.
FREMONT AVE.
FREMONT RD.
WRIGHT AVE.
SPOKANE GARRY DR
GOVERNMENT WAY
OWENS RIDGE

4000 WEST RANDOLPH ROAD
SPOKANE, WASHINGTON 99204
PHONE (509) 328-2971 (FOOD SERVICE 327-3441)
FAX (509) 325-6540

FOOTNOTES

1. *Spokesman Review* (Spokane, Washington, January 1, 1897.

2. *Spokesman Review*, November 29, 1894. This quoted statement may reflect a somewhat desperate attempt to relieve a trying economic situation. It would be difficult to accept that a newspaper reporter could not envision even one disadvantage.

3. *Spokesman Review*, January 1, 1897. According to the *Spokesman Review* of December 7, 1897, the Spokane Bureau of Immigration wrote to General Elwell P. Otis in the early Spring, 1894. Although the offer of land on Peone Prairie and documentation were forwarded to the War Department, no action was forthcoming.

4. *Spokesman Review*, February 6, 1895; the *Spokesman Review* of December 7, 1894 stated that an amount of 125,000 gallons daily was adopted by City Resolution.

5. Department of the Army, Center for Military History, *File HRC 331*, Fort George Wright, Washington; *Army and Navy Journal*, November 3, 1894, page 153. Brigadier General Carlin, Commander of the Department of the Columbia, had recommended construction of a fort near Spokane in 1893.

6. *Spokesman Review*, December 7, 1894, January 1, 1897, December 21, 1894; Center for Military History, *File HRC 331*. It should be noted that even as these plans were proposed for posts in Spokane and in Helena, Montana, the War Department also had in mind a still larger post, costing about $2 million, to be located in the Puget Sound area; *Army and Navy Journal*. April 4, 1896; *Spokesman Review*, February 10, 1895.

7. *Spokesman Review*, August 15, 1895.

8. *Spokesman Review*, November 29, 1894.

9. Mary Ellen Rowe, "Fort George Wright, Washington 1894-1912: A Case Study in Civilian-Military Relations Before the First World War," Master Thesis, University of Washington, 1980, p. 13; *Spokesman Review*, December 2, 1894.

10. *Spokesman Review*, December 2, 7, 20, 1894. For the first two years of his enlistment, a private earned $13 per month with increases of one dollar per month for each year of service between the third and fifth year, and then $16 per month after that. The $16 per month continued during the next five years of continuous service. At the eleventh year, his pay

climbed to $18 per month for the next five years, with $1 per month for each subsequent five years of continuous service.

Corporals and duty sergeants experienced the same pay schedule as the privates, but with $15.00 and $20.00 per month starting pay. Sergeants made $25.00-30.00 per month. When enlisted men were on active duty during war time, they received an additional twenty per cent pay.

11. *Spokesman Review*, December 1, 1894; February 12, 15, 1895; March 7, 1895.

12. *Spokesman Review*, December 19, 1894. Several issues of the newspaper during March, 1895 contain lists of those who made donations of cash and property to secure the military post for Spokane. See appendixes C an D.

13. *Spokesman Review*, November 30, 1894; February 8, 12, 1895.

14. *Spokesman Review*, December 1, 2, 4, 1894.

15. *Spokesman Review*, December 5, 7, 1894. The concert took place on December 6, 1894.

16. *Spokesman Review*, December 9, 16, 29, 1894. The distribution of the Christmas Tree Entertainment donations occurred on New Year's Eve, 1894; the auction, on February 6, 1895.

17. *Spokesman Review*, January 19, 1895; December 21, 1894; *Army and Navy Journal*, August 17, 1895.

18. *Army and Navy Journal*, March 30, 1895.

19. A recent book, *Sentinel of Silence*, by David Chance (Pacific Northwest National Parks Association, 1981) provides useful information about Fort Spokane, troops garrisoned there, and local Indian people.

20. *Spokesman Review*, January 9, 1895; February 27, 1895; March 19, 1895.

21. *Spokesman Review*, April 18, 1895; May 30, 1895; Office of the Judge Advocate General, *U.S. Military Reservations, National Cemeteries, and Military Parks*, rev. ed., Washington, D.C., 1907, p. 392 in Rowe, Fort George Wright, p. 15.

22. *Spokesman Review*, February 10, 1895.

23. *Spokesman Review*, August 25, 1896. The structural organization of the United States Army in the earlier years of Fort George Wright was as follows: a brigade was composed of three regiments, each of which a Colonel commanded. A regiment, comprising three

battalions, had each battalion headed by a Major. Each battalion consisted of four companies which were each in charge of a Captain, assisted by two lieutenants. A company was subdivided into platoons and squads, which were under the command of lieutenants, sergeants, and corporals. *Army and Navy Journal*, November 30, 1895.

24. *Spokesman Review*, December 31, 1896; January 1, 1897; *Army and Navy Journal*, February 27, 1897.

25. The unsavory quality of the Spokane River for domestic purposes was hinted at rather broadly in a newspaper story which stated that the Fort, being downstream from the city, would not use river water in the homes.

26. *Spokesman Review*, February 15, April 20, May 1, 1897. It is interesting to note that there was no ground-breaking ceremony at Fort Wright when construction began at the site in 1897.

27. *Spokesman Review*, January 4, 7, February 15, 1897; December 31, 1896.

28. *Spokesman Review*, July 4, November 5, 1897; Rowe *Fort George Wright*, p. 23.

29. *Spokesman Review*, August 13, 1897. Keefe was prepared to set up a brick kiln if there were not brickyards in Spokane. However, the manufacture of bricks was an early enterprise in Spokan Falls as the *Spokan Times* of June 26, 1879 reported. The *Fort Wright College Historical Museum Tour Information and Business Guide* (page 21) stated that bricks for the post were made at the Gladding McBean Company. No source for this information was included. However, Mr. (J.T.) Davie received the contract for bricks, according to the *Spokesman Review* of April 9, 1898. Davie had a brickyard in the Hangman Creek area as early as 1883 (*Spokan Falls Chronicle*, July 7, 1883).

30. *Spokesman Review* June 26, July 9, August 13, 1897. Terms of the contract for the sewer system required laying 11,156 lineal feet of 8 inch vitrified sewer pipe, costing 40 cents per foot, and laying 621 feet of galvanized iron pipe at 20 cents per foot from water mains to flush tanks, build manholes, lampholes, lay branches and ties, excavate, and back-fill.

The water system called for the following: 8976 lineal feet of 6 inch cast iron pipe, valves, crosses, ties, and hydrants at 21.5 cents per foot; 2676 lineal feet of 4 inch cast iron pipe at 21.33 cents per foot; 1600 lineal feet of ¾ inch galvanized blow-off pipe, including gate valves, trenches, and back-filling at 14 cents per foot.

31. *Spokesman Review*, July 22, September 15, 30, 1897.

32. *Spokesman Review*, August 28, 1897. The brick mason collected 5 cents of the fare — in midstream — each way.

33. *Spokesman Review*, May 1, August 10, November 5, 1897.

34. *Spokesman Review*, April 16, 1897; Center for Military History, *File HRC 331*, p. 30.

35. *Spokesman Review*, June 13, 1897.

36. *Spokesman Review*, June 11, 1897.

37. *Spokesman Review*, August 16, 28, 1897. See Appendix A for a listing of the buildings still existing at Fort George Wright, the completion date of the construction, and costs of each building.

38. *Spokesman Review* September 16, 1898. Water Pollution was not a public issue at this time. Nonetheless, Post Surgeon T.G. Holmes foresaw the potential for a typhoid epidemic and complained vigorously to Spokane health authorities about the garbage in the river. Rowe records the exchange between these two men in her thesis, page 32; *Army and Navy Journal*, January 30, 1897.

39. Rowe, *Fort George Wright*, p. 52. Rowe discusses the Black troops in Spokane in detail, pp. 49-74. Jack Foner, in his study of U.S. soldiers in the period between World War I and World War II states that prejudice toward Black soldiers from the communities in which they were stationed brought about a level of cohesiveness among the enlisted men and a high retention rate. In a more general way, George A. Forsyth, *The Story of the Soldier*, states that cohesion among troops was typically strong in companies because its members seldom sought associates elsewhere, not due to any anomosity "but because each is sufficient to itself." (pp. 126-127).

Foner goes on to say that this cohesiveness enabled a majority of enlisted men and non-commissioned officers to become well-trained, highly skilled, easily meeting the demands of the Army and is illustrated by an episode in the Philippines by a force of 350 men of the 24th Infantry, led by Captain Joseph B. Batchelor, a later commander at Fort George Wright. They "marched over 300 miles without any guides in unknown territory, following trails that were just passable through chilling nights and sweltering days; made 123 deep fords; . . . crossed 80 miles of precipitous mountains in five days . . . ; lived three weeks on unaccustomed and insufficient food; and in the end forced the surrender of more than 1,000 without mistreating anyone." (Jack Foner, *The United States Soldier Between Two Wars*, pp. 6-10 in Marvin Fletcher, *The Black Soldier and Officer in the United States Army, 1894-1917*, pp. 51-52). See also, William G. Muller, *The 24th Infantry, Past and Present*, n.p.

40. Muller, *The 24th Infantry*, n.p. The 24th Infantry, whose Company "M" was the first detachment stationed at Fort Wright, had a second tour of duty in the Philippines, arriving there in 1906. Residents of Manila had fond memories of a series of popular entertainments the soldiers presented while on their first assignments in the Islands. Captain Moss, regiment adjutant and aide-de-camp to General Corbin, supported and encouraged their performances.

Manila American, February 20, 1906 in *The 24th Infantry*, n.p.

41. Rowe, *Fort George Wright*, p. 52; Katz, *The Black West*, pp. 203-204; Leckie, *The Buffalo Soldiers*, pp. 258-59.

42. Muller, the 24th Infantry, n.p. It should be noted that as a young lieutenant, John J. Pershing led a company of the 10th Cavalry, a Black unit, in Montana, Mexico, and Puerto Rico, earning the name "Black Jack." (see Katz, *The Black West*, pp. 201-202).

Nelson A. Miles, who years later, with General O.O. Howard accepted Nez Perce Chief Joseph's surrender in Montana's Bear Paw Mountains, commanded the 40th regiment of colored troops from July, 1866 to March, 1869, which with the 39th regiment formed the 25th Infantry by an act of Congress on March 3, 1869. The 25th Infantry served at Fort George Wright in 1908-1912.

Some years after George Armstrong Custer refused assignment to command Black soldiers, Brigadier General James Parker gained the hostility of General Wallace Randolph, Acting Chief of Artillery, because Parker had written in a memorandum the suggestion that "in the reconstitution of the field artillery the artillery have their share of colored soldiers then confined to the infantry and cavalry." Randolph resented the suggestion. (James Parker, The Old Army, pp. 390-91).

43. Rowe, *Fort George Wright*, p. 50.

44. *Spokane Chronicle*, August 22, 1900 in Rowe, *Fort George Wright*, pp. 63-64.

45. Katz, *The Black West*, p. 219.

46. Muller, the 24th Infantry, n.p.

47. This was the 25th Infantry that arrived in 1908. The 25th Infantry Band, composed of Black soldiers, entertained at the 1904 St. Louis World's Fair where they were acknowledged as one of the best bands in the United States. See also Rowe, *Fort George Wright*, p. 42. The Washington Water Powser Company diversified its holdings in 1895 by incorporating Twickenham Park as an amusement park, naming it Natatorium Park for the large swimming pool, or natatorium located there.

48. Undated clipping, Fort George Wright Scrapbook, Fairchild Heritage Museum, Fairchild Air Force Base, Spokane, Washington.

49. *Spokesman Review*, August 26, 1910; Ruby El Hult, *Northwest Disaster*, p. 104. According to the August, 1910 *Post Returns*, Companies "M," "E," "H," "I," and "K," of the 25th Infantry were recalled from maneuvers at American Lake for fire-fighting duty.

50. Hult, *Northwest Disaster*, pp. 104, 113, 133, 160, 166. The companies from Fort George Wright worked from the following locations to help control the fires: Company "E" —

McDonald, Montana, Company "G" — Avery, Idaho, Company "H" — Dixon, Montana, Company "I" — Wallace, Idaho, Company "K" — Essex, Montana, Company "L" — Yack, Montana, Company "M" — Belton, Montana.

51. Hult, *Northwest Disaster*, pp. 160, 190.

52. John H. Nankivell, *The History of the Twenty-Fifth Regiment United States Infantry 1869-1926*, p. 134.

53. F.W. Warren Air Force Base, Air Force Regional Civil Engineer-Ballistic Missile Support, *Architectural History, Volume I*, September, 1984, pp. 3-17.

54. *Spokesman Review*, January 15, 1899.

55. *Ibid.*; Fort George Wright, *Building Repair Records*, Spokane, Washington copies, Author's possession.

56. *Spokesman Review*, January 15, 1899; February 20, 1911. It was the Office of the Surgeon General, not the Quartermaster General's Office, that usually supplied the blueprints for hospitals on base, as well as for other medical facilities. The original hospital at Fort George Wright measured 46ft. 3in. by 54ft. 11in. The four storey addition of 27ft 3in. by 48ft. 4in. added about 5000 square feet to the structure.

57. Mary Elizabeth Dunton, SNJM and Patsy Garrett, *Application* to the National Register of Historic Places. Fort George Wright was accepted for inclusion in the National Register of Historic Places as an Historic District in May, 1976.
According to Jane R. Kendall in her article "History of Fort Francis E. Warren (*Annals of Wyoming*, Volume 18, p. 55) Fort D.A. Russell/F.E. Warren is known as "a monument to pork barrel legislation" with over $7 million spent to expand and equip it. Senator Warren was enormously successful obtaining both construction and maintenance appropriations for Fort Russell, beginning in 1892 and continuing for many years thereafter.

58. Forsyth, *The Story of the Soldier*, p. 111.

59. The duplex for lieutenants was not completed until 1906. See Appendix A for specific information.

60. Rowe, *Fort George Wright*, pp 82-83.

61. As early as July 22, 1899, the *Army and Navy Journal* editorially lamented that the post was not named Fort George Wright.

62. *Spokesman Review*, February 12, September 26, 1902. The President of the United States

had decreed that a regiment of Infantry would be organized as follows: 65 enlisted men assigned to one company (12 companies to the regiment) for a total of 780 men. The composition of a Company consisted of a First Sergeant, a Quartermaster Sergeant, four Sergeants, Six Corporals, two Cooks, two Musicians, one Artificer, and 48 Privates for a total of 65 men. The regimental and battalion NCO staff would be comprised of eight men while the regimental Band had twenty-eight men. The Infantry Band had 12 Privates, one Cook, eight Corporals, four Sergeants, one Drum Major Principal Musician, and one Chief Musician. These different capacities totalled 816 enlisted men in the regiment. With 30 regiments in the Infantry, there were 24,482 enlisted men in the Infantry in 1902. (Heitman, *Historical Register*, p. 625).

63. *Spokesman Review*, April 15, 1903.

64. *Spokesman Review*, March 27, 1903.

65. Undated clippings, *Fort George Wright Scrapbook*, n.p.; *Spokesman Review*, February 13, 1903.

66. *Ibid.*

67. Fort George Wright, *Post Returns* April, 1901, December, 1906.

68. *Spokesman Review*, December 25, 1903.

69. *Spokesman Review*, February 15, 1904; February 11, 1905.

70. *Spokesman Review*, August 8, 1911, October 14, 1909. In 1911, enlisted men received between $15 and $70 monthly, depending upon their rank. This amounted to a payroll of almost $20,000 each month at the Spokane post.

71. *Spokesman Review*, March 9, 1904, November 6, 1903, February 20, 1911. When Fort George Wright was declared surplus to government need in the late 1950's, Fairchild Air Force Base still counted on Fort wright as the source of some of its water supply.

72. Rowe, Fort George Wright, pp. 31-32.

73. *Spokesman Review*, January 27, 1906.

74. *Spokesman Review*, March 2, 1905.

75. *Spokesman Review* in Rowe, *Fort George Wright*, p. 36.

76. Spokane seems to have forgotten an item carried in the February 10, 1895 issue of the *Spokesman Review* which reported that the War Department, in addition to posts in Spokane and in Helena Montana, also intended to construct a still larger post in the future somewhere

on Puget Sound, costing approximately $2 million (in 1895 values).

77. Undated clipping, *Fort George Wright Scrapbook*, n.p.

78. Fort George Wright, *Post Returns, Records of Events*, November, 1906, April 1908; undated clipping *Fort George Wright Scrapbook*, n.p. Fort Lawton in Seattle, situated on 700 acres of prime Magnolia Bluff land overlooking Salmon Bay in Puget Sound, was authorized and established in June, 1898. Workers completed the first phase of building in 1900. Like Fort George Wright, Fort Lawton never became the regimental post Seattle citizens dreamed of.

79. *Spokesman Review*, April 21, 1908; undated clipping, *Fort George Wright Scrapbook*, n.p.

80. *Ibid*. On still another occasion, 4th Infantry troops participated in an annual pioneer celebration, dressed as Lewis and Clark expedition members, traders, trappers, mountain men, pioneers, etc., authorized by Colonel Joseph K. Partello, commander at Fort George Wright.

81. Parker, *The Old Army*, pp. 393-394. The Army Relief Society formed during the winter of 1898-1899 as the result of a refusal to a lady by Army generals. General Leonard Wood and General Francis N. Greene endorsed a fair in New York City which benefitted Cubans left destitute due to the Spanish-American War. The wife of Brigadier General James Parker asked for one day's receipts per week for the relief of widows and orphans of soldiers and officers who had died in that war. The Generals could not see their way to do as Mrs. Parker requested.

Mrs. Parker was obviously a woman with a cause and did not accept "no" from Army brass. She gathered a nucleus of friends — among them the wife of Secretary of War Lamont — and went about organizing an Army Relief Society. This group contacted friends at posts throughout the country, as well as non-military acquaintances, and soon "sections" formed, each of which contributed no less than $25.00. With a mere $15.00 in its treasury, the organization quickly grew to the point that it engaged a Wall Street firm — Morgan, Bliss and Lamont — to audit its accounts. The Army Relief Society through the years has accomplished much to benefit its own.

82. *Spokesman Review*, April 20, 27, 1908. The original bandstand at Fort George Wright came from Fort Sherman in Coeur d'Alene, Idaho.

83. Fort George Wright, *Building Repair Records*. Although all officers received library tables on the same delivery date — October 10, 1908 — all, except the Bachelor Officers Quarters received dining room extension tables at that time. The married officers' residences were furnished with dining room arm chairs and side chairs just before the Christmas holidays that same year. However, these chairs and the extension tables did not reach the Bachelor's residence until July, 1909.

84. *Spokesman Review*, February 12, 1909.

85. Parker, *The Old Army*, pp. 405-407.

86. *Spokesman Review*, August 8, December 20, 1911.

87. *Spokesman Review*, November 28, 1903.

88. Undated clipping, Fort George Wright Scrapbook, n.p.; Lawr. V. Salo, *Cultural Resource Reconnaissance*, U.S. Corps of Engineers, Seattle District, 1986, pp. 8, 11.

89. Undated clipping, *Fort George Wright Scrapbook*, n.p.

90. *Ibid.*

91. *Ibid.*

92 *Spokesman Review*, November 28, 1903; January 24, 1911.

93. In the latter six months of 1899, there were 34 civilians working at Fort George Wright. Their number increased to 98 the following year.

94. *Spokesman Review*, October 16, 1911.

95. Nankivell, *History of the Twenty-Fifth*, pp. 163-164.

96. *Ibid.*

97. Nankivell, *History of the Twenty Fifth*, p. 167.

98. *Spokesman Review*, December 19, 1911. The International Committee of the YMCA was authorized to establish their work among regular and volunteer soldiers at Fort George Wright in 1899. The "Y" held services on the post each Sunday.

99. *Spokesman Review*, June 8, 1912.

100. Fort George Wright, *Post Returns*, January-December, 1908. In 1908 when the 24th Infantry received orders to depart from the Philippines for the United States, enlisted men known to be of very good character were given the option of transferring to other colored units in the Islands, if they had at least six months to serve before discharge from the Army. If their service time was less than six months in duration, they could be granted the privilege of discharge and immediate re-enlistment.

101. *Some Facts About Our Army and Fort George Wright, Washington*, Shaw-Borden Company, Spokane, Washington, 1913, pp. 23, 25.

102. *Spokesman Review*, January 26, 1916.

103. Nankivell, *History of the Twenty-Fifth*, p. 143.

104. *Spokesman Review*, January 8, 1921.

105. *Spokesman Review*, September 20, 1933; *Fort George Wright CCC Annual*, 1937, pp. 3, 7; *CCC in Washington State Parks*, Washington State Parks and Recreation Commission, Olympia, Washington, June, 1988. See Appendix B for a list of CCC camps in the Fort George Wright District. Communication with these widely-dispersed camps was facilitated by the establishment of a CCC Radio School at the CCC District Headquarters at Fort George Wright in 1935. The tax-payers were saved over $5000 in costs, compared to using telephone and telegraph services.

106. Interviews with Colonel George S. Clarke (ret.) at his Spokane, Washington home, by Eileen Polich (May 15, 1964; by Patricia Cevil (May 8, 1964); and by Sister M. Andrea Rose (May 8, 1964).

107. *Ibid.*

108. Interview with Colonel George S. Clarke (ret.) by Sister M. Andrea Rose, May 8, 1964.

109. *Spokesman Review*, September 20, 1933; undated clipping, *Fort George Wright Scrapbook*, n.p.

110. Forsyth, *The Story of the Soldier*, p. 96.

111. Undated clipping, *Fort George Wright Scrapbook*, n.p.

112. Undated clipping, *Fort George Wright Scrapbook*, n.p.

113. Undated clipping, *] ort George Wright Scrapbook*, n.p.

114. Undated clipping, *Fort George Wright Scrapbook*, n.p.

115. Undated clippings, *Fort George Wright Scrapbook*, Fort George Files, Fairchild Air Force Base, Washington.

116. Undated clipping, *Fort George Wright Scrapbook*, n.p.

117. Undated clipping, *Fort George Wright Scrapbook*, n.p.

118. *Spokane Chronicle*, October 28, 1939.

119. *Spokesman Review*, June 29, July 10, 1941.

120. *Spokesman Review*, June 19, 1940; Victor L. Mantese, "Fossils of the Fourth Infantry," *Spokesman Review*, July 5, 1964.

121. *Spokesman Review*, June 19, 1940; *Letter*, March 22, 1941 from L.E. Ostrander, Adjutant General, War Department, Washington, D.C. to Commanding Generals, GHQ Air Force and Fourth and Ninth Corps Areas; *Spokesman Review*, June 10, 1943, July 10, 1967. The Second Air Force had responsibility for the development and supervision of about 30 bases in the west, and east to the state of Nebraska. Each of these bases was a training site for combat crews whose next assignment would be actual combat.

122. N.C. Christense, "Ghosts of Wartime Agency Haunt Fort Wright," *Spokesman Review*, January 21, 1962.

123. *Spokesman Review*, March 25, 1902, August 17, 1903; AAF Convalescent Hospital *Review*, Fort George Wright, Washington, February, 1945, n.p., September, 1944, n.p.

124. AAF *Review* February, 1945, n.p. Through the efforts of the Spokane Chamber of Commerce Agricultural Committee a course in animal husbandry came into being at the base. Patients cared for the various farm animals and riding horses. This program was especially helpful because in subtle ways it focused on life and living.

125. *Review*, September, 1944, n.p.

126. *Ibid.*

127. AAF Convalescent Hospital, Fort George Wright, Washington, *The Review Weekly*, February 24, 1945, p. 2.

128. This area is called Hi-Bridge or High Bridge.

129. *Minutes*, Board of Regents, Washington State College, July 22, 23, 1946 (including Exhibit "G" memorandum, July 16, 1946); *Spokesman Review*, July 13, 1946. The *Spokesman Review* reported in its September 7, 1946 edition that War Department commitments to Washington State College regarding use of some of the buildings for dormitories and classrooms would be honored despite that the 15th Air Force was to move to Fort George

Wright on November 1, of that year.

130. *Minutes*, Board of Regents, Washington State College, December 16-17, 1949.

131. *Spokesman Review*, April 20, 1960.

132. *Minutes*, Board of Regents, Washigton State University, August, September, 1960. (The College became a University on September 1, 1959).

133. Oral interviews with Celine Steinberger, SNJM, Autumn, 1987.

134. *Minutes*, Advisory Board, Holy Names Center at Fort Wright, Spokane, Washington, December, 1984 to September, 1989.

135. *Fort Wright Properties*, Holy Names Center at Fort Wright, Spokane, Washington, December, 1985; *Final Report, Fort Wright Properties*, Development Information Packet, NBBJ Group, Seattle, Washington, December, 1985.

136. *Letter* to Celine Steinberger, SNJM, Executive Director Holy Names Center at Fort Wright from Yasufumi Kajiwara, Principal, Mukogawa Senior High School, September 4, 1987.

FORT GEORGE WRIGHT: NOT ONLY WHERE THE BAND PLAYED

BIBLIOGRAPHY

Air Force Regional Civil Engineer-Ballistic Missile Support. *Architectural Survey, Volume 1, Architectural History*. F.E. Warren Air Force Base (Wyoming), September, 1984.

--------. *Installation Planning and Design Guide*. F.E. Warren Air Force Base (Wyoming), April, 1984.

Army and Navy Journal, 1892-1898.

Army Air Force. *Fort George Wright Review*. Base Headquarters, Fort George Wright, Spokane, Washington, April 16, 1943, May 29, 1943, June 24, 1943.

--------. *Review*. Convalescent Hospital Fort George Wright. Spokane, Washington, September through December, 1944; January, February, April, 1945.

--------. *Review*. Regional and Convalescent Hospital Fort George Wright, Spokane, Washington, August, 1945.

--------. *The Review Weekly*. Convalescent Hospital Fort George Wright, Spokane, Washington, February 24, 1945.

Baker, Bruce. "Gone But Not Forgotten: Fort George Wright Hospital in the 1940s." *Medical Bulletin*, Spokane County Medical Society, Spokane, Washington, FAll, 1989, pp. 26-29.

Bulletin. Sisters of the Holy Names, Development Department, Spokane, Washington, October, 1984.

CCC District Headquarters. *Fort George Wright CCC Annual*. CCC District Headquarters, Fort George Wright, Spokane, Washington, 1937.

Chance David, *Sentinel of Silence*, N.P. Pacific Northwest National Parks Association, 1981.

Christensen, N.C. "Ghosts of Wartime Agency Haunt Fort Wright." *Spokesman Review*, January 21, 1962.

"Court Stops Ft. Lawton Razing: Some Buildings Go." *Headquarters Heliogram*, Council on America's Military Past, January/February, 1988.

Department of the Army. *Files -HRC-331- Fort George Wright*. Center for Military History, Washington, D.C., n.d.

Dunton, Mary Elizabeth, SNJM and Patsy Garrett. *Application to the National Register of Historic Places*. Washington, D.C.(adopted) May, 1976.

Architecture, Washington State University, Pullman, Washington, May, 1985.

Memo. Sisters of the Holy Names, Washington Province, Spokane, Washington, September 20, 1984.

Muller, William G. *The Twenty-Fourth Infantry, Past and Present* (a re-issue). Fort Collins, Colorado, Old Army Press, 1972.

Nankivell, John H. (editor and compiler). *History of the Twenty-Fifth Regiment United States Infantry 1869-1926.* Denver, Colorado, Smith Brooks Printing, 1969 (reprinted).

National Historic Landmark: Francis E. Warren. N.p., n.p., n.d.

NBBJ Group. *Final Report, Development Information Packet.* NBBJ Group, Seattle, Washington, December, 1985.

--------. *Fort Wright Properties, Developers Information Packet.* NBBJ Group, Seattle, Washington, December, 1985.

Office of the Judge Advocate General. *U.S. Military Reservations, National Cemeteries and Military Parks,* rev. ed., Washington, D.C., 1907.

Parker, James. *The Old Army — Memories, 1872-1918.* Philadelphia: Dorrance & Company, 1929.

Post Returns. Fort George Wright, Spokane, Washington, 1891-1908.

Rowe, Mary Ellen. "Fort George Wright, Spokane, Washington, 1894-1912: A Case study in Civilian-Military Relations Before the First World War." Unpublished Masters Thesis, University of Washington, 1980.

Salo, Lawr. V. *Cultural Resource Reconnaissance.* Department of the Army, U.S. Corps of Engineers, Seattle District, Seattle, Washington, 1986.

"Seattle Starts Razing of Ft. Lawton Buildings." *Headquarters Heliogram,* Council on America's Military Past, September/October, 1987.

Some Facts About Our Army and Fort George Wright, Washington. Shaw-Borden Company, Spokane, Washington, 1913.

Spokane Chronicle. Spokane, Washington, 1883, 1891-1960.

Spokan Times. Spokane, Washington, 1879-1882.

Spokesman Review. Spokane, Washington, 1894-1960.

Sullivan, Charles J. *Army Posts and Towns: The Bedeker of the Army*. Burlington, Vermont, Free Press Interstate Printing Corp., 1935.

United States Department of Agriculture. *When the Mountains Roared, Stories of 1910 Fire*. Forest Service — Idaho Panhandle National Forests, n.p., n.d.

War Department. *Military Reservations — Washington State, 1937-42*. Government Printing Office, Washington, D.C., n.d.

Washington State College. *Board of Regents Minutes*. Washington State College, Pullman, Washington, July, 1946; December, 1949.

Washington State Parks and Recreation Commission. *CCC in Washington State Parks*. Olympia, Washington, June, 1988.

Washington State University. *Board of Regents Minutes*. Washington State University, Pullman, Washington, September, 1960; April, 1961.

Quartermaster's Garage: Another 1920 vintage building was this wood Quartrmaster's garage. It could accept 16 vehicles for storage or parking.

FORT GEORGE WRIGHT: NOT ONLY WHERE THE BAND PLAYED

Barracks Headquarters CCC: This unpretentious building served as barracks for the CCC Headquarters Company at Fort George Wright. Resting on concrete piers, this 1985 sq. ft. structure was built in November, 1934.

District Headquarters Building: Fort Geroge Wright served as headquarters for the largest CCC District in the United States. Administrative offices housed in this 5,132 sq. ft. building oversaw thousands of CCC enrolles in four states.

Stables: This wood structure, the second stables at the site, was 160 feet long. Completed in 1920, it had a capacity of 40 animals.

Officers' Duplex: Completed early in 1906, this residence was intended to be occupied by Lieutenants and their families. Each side had 1700 sq. ft. of living space.

Polo Club: Now a part of the Spokane Falls Community College, this handsome building overlooks a valley of the Spokane River. Built of logs, squared on three sides, the 1939 structure had a cedar shake roof and a flagstone porch.

Post Hospital: An imposing building, the post hospital was added onto in 1911 so that it had a capacity of 56 beds. Not including the basement, there were 11.312 sq. ft. in the building. It burned to the ground in 1967.

Guardhouse: The guardhouse, built in 1908, housed 34 prisoners when each cell was used. Built at a cost of $21,561, the building measured 47 ft. x 87 ft. It no longer stands at Fort Wright.

NCO Residence: A later NCO residence was this 800 sq. ft. building, completed late in 1922 at a cost of $250.00

Hospital Steward's Quarters: Another of the early buildings at Fort George Wright, this building was occupied by one non-commissioned officer. Reflecting other structures at the site, this home cost $2400 to build. It stands across Fort George Wright Drive from the former post.

Service Club and Gymnasium: Once the location of gala parties and dignified receptions, this imposing building was, in part, the result of efforts by the Spokane Chamber of Commerce lobbying Washington's Congressional delegates. Completed in January, 1905, it had 4,355 sq. ft. of space. It no longer exists at the site.

Commissary Warehouse: The commissary warehouse was an early building at Fort Wright. Like other structures, it had red brick walls, a stone foundation, and a slate roof. Warmed by a coal fired steam furnace, it was completed in April, 1903.

NCO Quarters: This modest 725 sq. ft. building was constructed in 1931.

Paint and Oil Storehouse: A depression era building, this 20 ft. x 50 ft. structure had a gravel floor, stone walls, and foundation. It was unheated and had a sheet metal roof.

Y

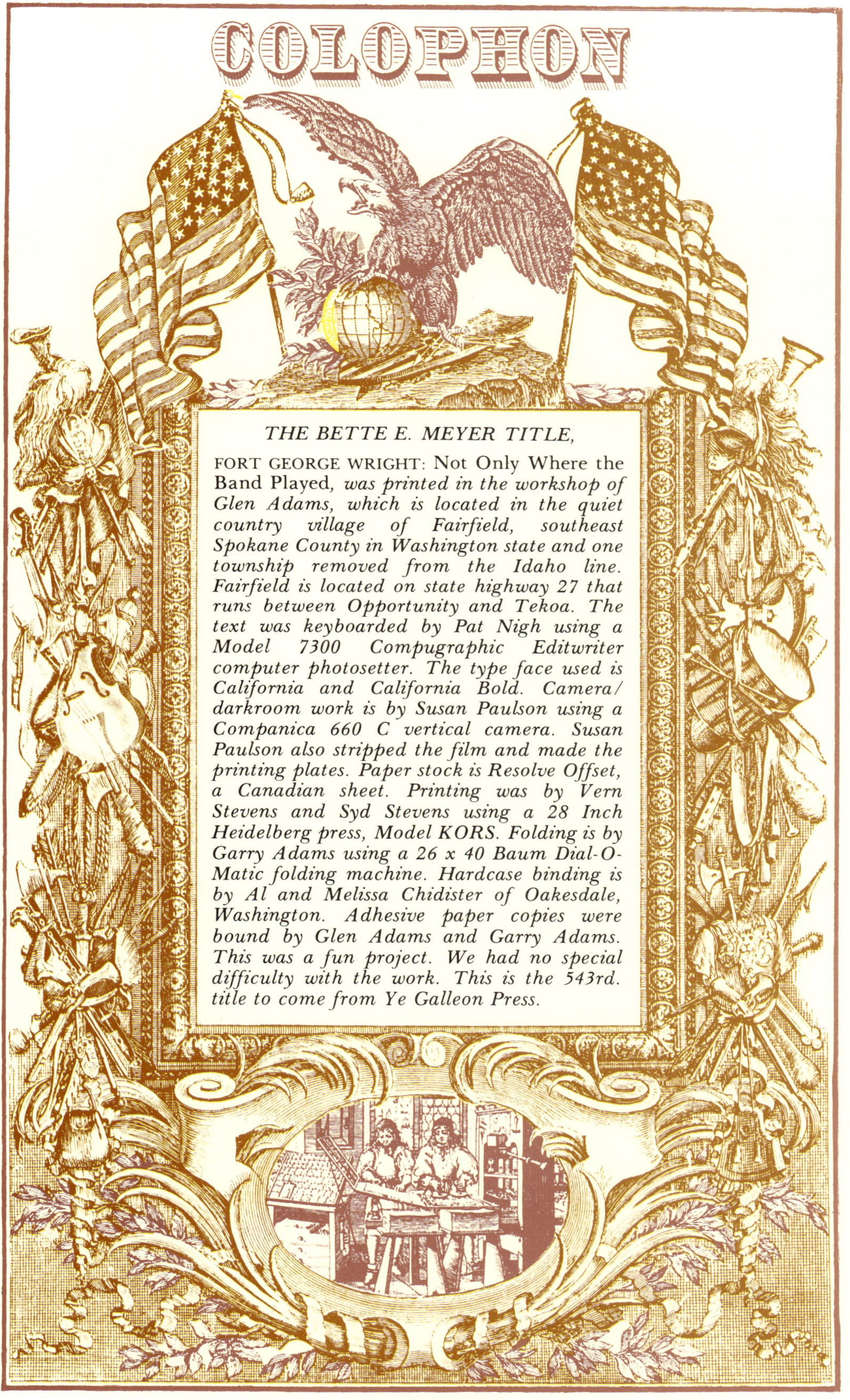

COLOPHON

THE BETTE E. MEYER TITLE,

FORT GEORGE WRIGHT: Not Only Where the Band Played, *was printed in the workshop of Glen Adams, which is located in the quiet country village of Fairfield, southeast Spokane County in Washington state and one township removed from the Idaho line. Fairfield is located on state highway 27 that runs between Opportunity and Tekoa. The text was keyboarded by Pat Nigh using a Model 7300 Compugraphic Editwriter computer photosetter. The type face used is California and California Bold. Camera/darkroom work is by Susan Paulson using a Companica 660 C vertical camera. Susan Paulson also stripped the film and made the printing plates. Paper stock is Resolve Offset, a Canadian sheet. Printing was by Vern Stevens and Syd Stevens using a 28 Inch Heidelberg press, Model KORS. Folding is by Garry Adams using a 26 x 40 Baum Dial-O-Matic folding machine. Hardcase binding is by Al and Melissa Chidister of Oakesdale, Washington. Adhesive paper copies were bound by Glen Adams and Garry Adams. This was a fun project. We had no special difficulty with the work. This is the 543rd. title to come from Ye Galleon Press.*

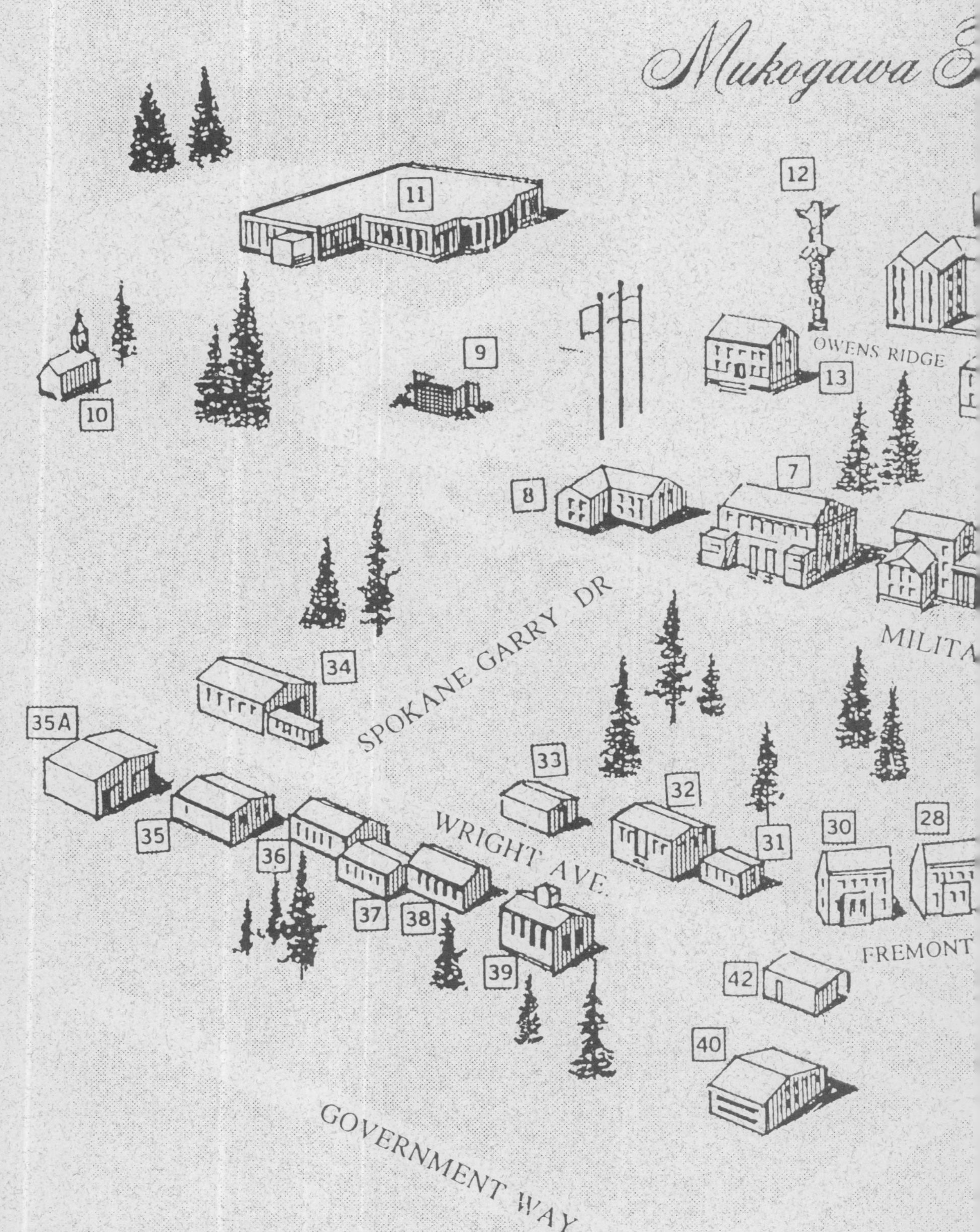

4000 WEST RANDOLPH ROAD
SPOKANE, WASHINGTON 99204
PHONE (509) 328-2971 (FOOD SERVICE 327-3441)
FAX (509) 325-6540

ℱort Wright Institute

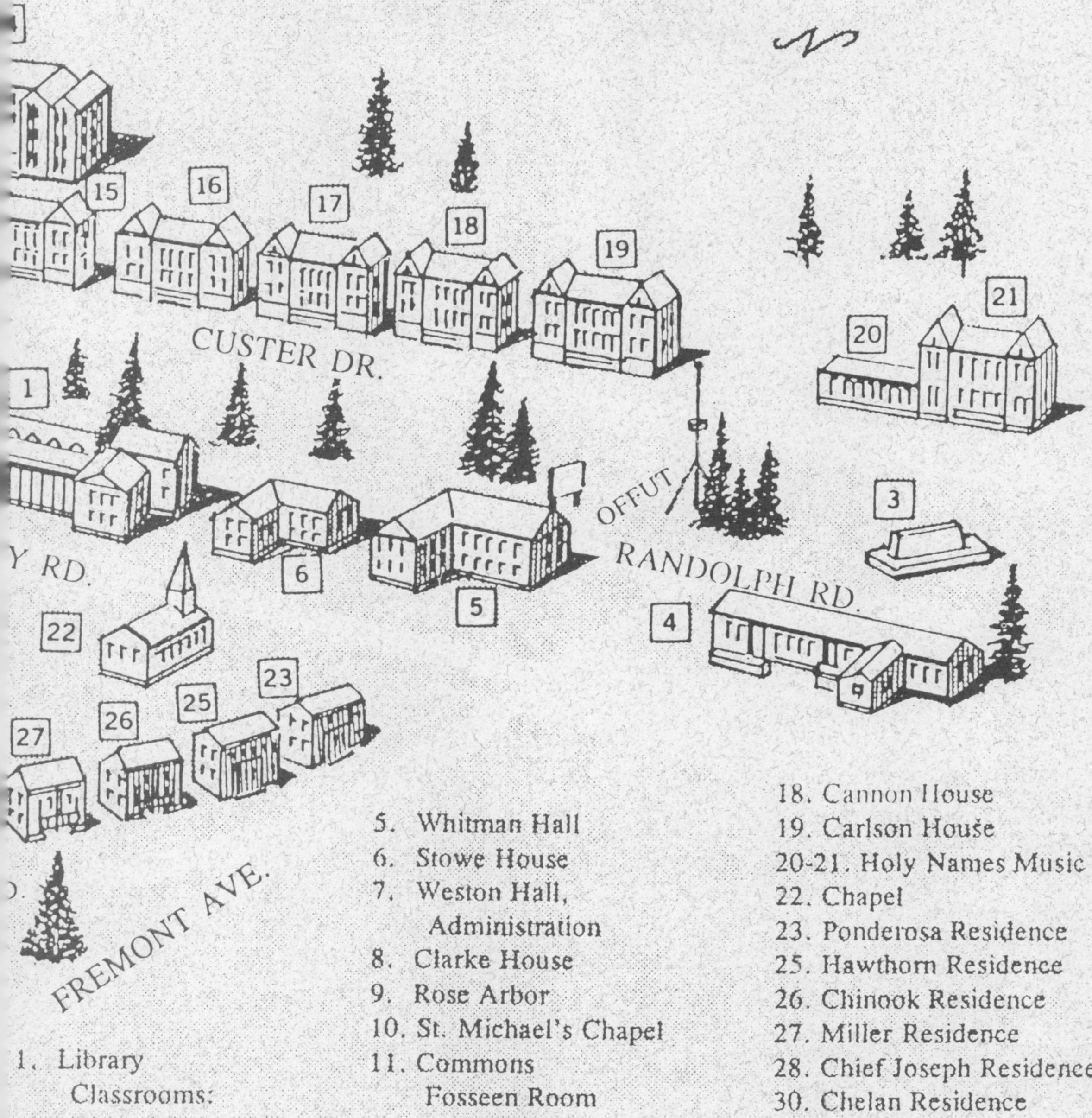

1. Library
   Classrooms:
   L201, L202, L203
   Audio Visual Room
   Computer Room
   Faculty Offices
3. Monument
4. Greystones
   Japanese C.C.
   Classrooms: CC1,2

5. Whitman Hall
6. Stowe House
7. Weston Hall,
   Administration
8. Clarke House
9. Rose Arbor
10. St. Michael's Chapel
11. Commons
    Fosseen Room
    Regents & Banquet Rooms
    Student Dining Hall
12. Totem Pole
13. Nellie Garry Guest Hse.
14. Covington Hall
15. Cather House
16. Dickinson House
17. Helen Keller House

18. Cannon House
19. Carlson House
20-21. Holy Names Music Ctr.
22. Chapel
23. Ponderosa Residence
25. Hawthorn Residence
26. Chinook Residence
27. Miller Residence
28. Chief Joseph Residence
30. Chelan Residence
31. Paint Shop
32. Toddler House
33. Art Gallery
34-35. Maintenance
36-38. MacDonald Clsrm. Bldg.
39. Stanton Classroom Bldg.
40. Montessori
42. Gas Station

CORPS OF ENGINEERS

U.S. ARMY

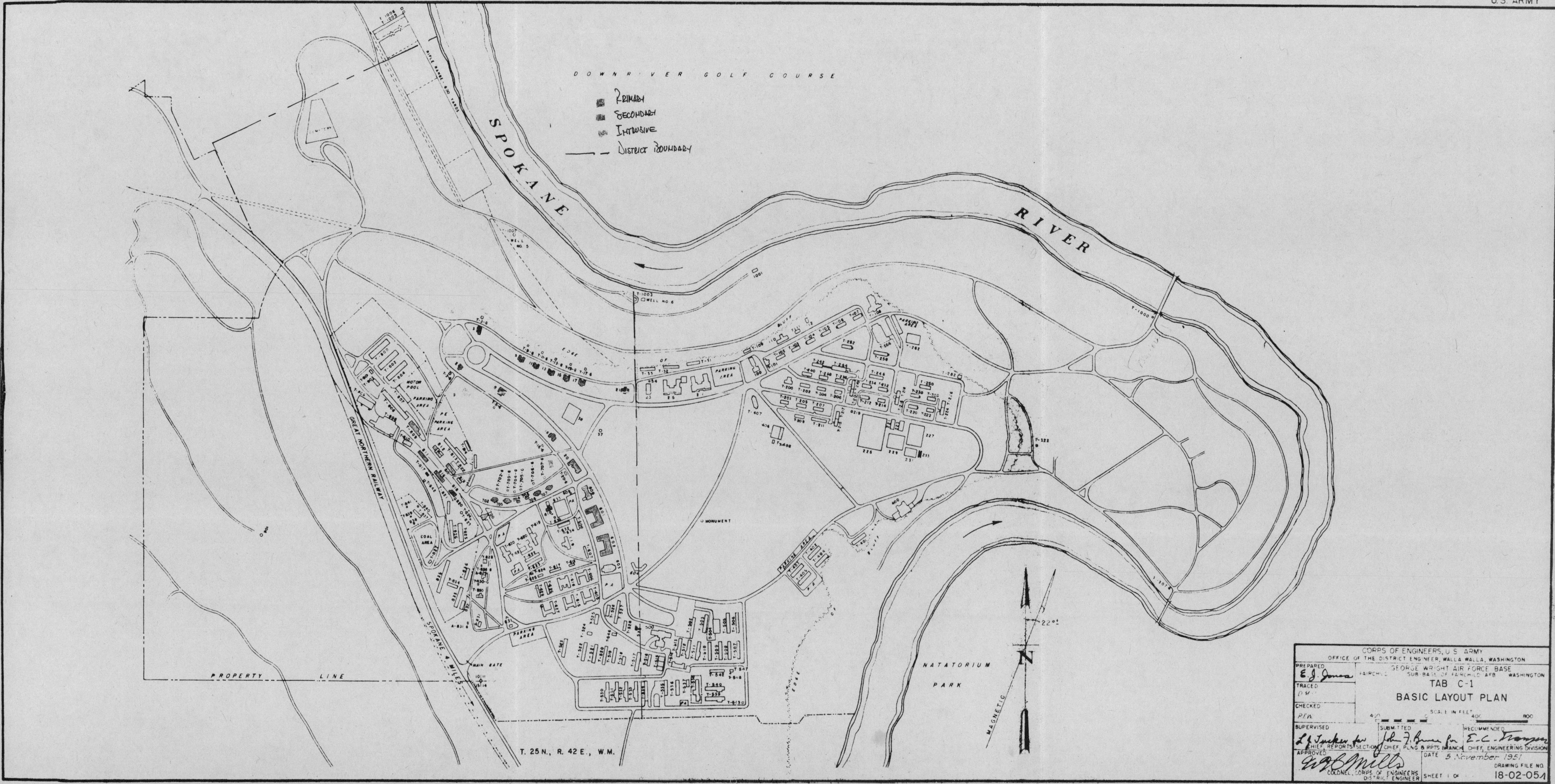
DOWNRIVER GOLF COURSE
Primary
Secondary
Intrusive
District Boundary
SPOKANE
RIVER
RIFLE RANGE - 630 YARDS
WELL NO. 5
WELL NO. 6
BLUFF
EDGE
PARKING AREA
MOTOR POOL
COAL AREA
MONUMENT
MAIN GATE
GREAT NORTHERN RAILWAY
SPOKANE 4 MILES
PROPERTY LINE
T. 25 N., R. 42 E., W.M.
NATATORIUM PARK
N
22°±
MAGNETIC
CORPS OF ENGINEERS, U.S. ARMY
OFFICE OF THE DISTRICT ENGINEER, WALLA WALLA, WASHINGTON
PREPARED
E. J. Jones
TRACED
CHECKED
P.F.W.
GEORGE WRIGHT AIR FORCE BASE
SUB-BASE OF FAIRCHILD AFB WASHINGTON
TAB C-1
BASIC LAYOUT PLAN
SCALE IN FEET
400 0 400 800
SUPERVISED
L. J. Tucker for
CHIEF, REPORTS SECTION
SUBMITTED
John J. Bruce for
CHIEF, PLNG & RPTS BRANCH
RECOMMENDED
E. C. Frangen
CHIEF, ENGINEERING DIVISION
APPROVED
COLONEL, CORPS OF ENGINEERS
DISTRICT ENGINEER
DATE 5 November 1951
SHEET 1 OF
DRAWING FILE NO.
18-02-051